Poison Ivy and Poison Oak

This weed (above) causes an itchy rash if you touch it. Poison Ivy grows like a vine, and Poison Oak grows like a shrub. Try to remember what the leaves look like, and do not touch it. If you do touch it, washing your hands as soon as possible may reduce the itching. Your local drug store will have various remedies that will help.

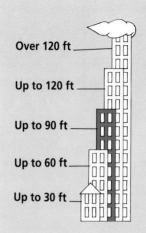

Over 120 ft

Up to 120 ft

Up to 90 ft

Up to 60 ft

Up to 30 ft

Tree Size Scale

This symbol is shown beside each tree. The red-colored section shows you at a glance how big the tree is likely to grow. However, young trees will be smaller than ones that are fully grown. In this example, the tree will be between 60 and 90 feet tall.

SCIENCE NATURE GUIDES

TREES
OF NORTH AMERICA

CONSULTANT
Alan Mitchell

IILLUSTRATIONS BY
David More

EDITED BY
Angela Royston

THUNDER BAY
P·R·E·S·S

Conservation

Trees are not only beautiful to look at. They clean the air and provide food and shelter for birds, squirrels, insects, and many other animals. When you are looking at trees, look for the wildlife that lives on them too.

City planners are well aware of the value of trees in towns and cities and you will find many different kinds growing there. Outside cities, however, trees and forests are still being cut down to clear land for building houses, shopping centers, and offices, and in the northwestern US for lumber.

Some of our finest trees are hundreds of years old and many of our forests have existed for over a thousand years. We now realize we must preserve them at all costs. On page 78, you will find the names of some organizations who campaign for the preservation of forests and the landscape. By joining them and supporting their efforts, you can help to preserve our trees and countryside.

Country Code

1 **Never break branches off a living tree** or carve your name in its bark.
2 **Don't climb trees**; you may damage them while you are doing so.
3 **Ask your parents only to light fires in a designated picnic area** in a wood or forest and use the fireplaces provided.
4 **Ask permission** before crossing private property.
5 **Keep to footpaths as much as possible** and don't trample the undergrowth.
6 **Leave fences and gates as you found them.**

Thunder Bay Press
5880 Oberlin Drive
Suite 400
San Diego, CA 92121

First published in the United States
by Thunder Bay Press, 1994

© Dragon's World, 1994
Text © Dragon's World, 1994
Illustrations © David More, 1994

Complete Cataloging in Publication (CIP) is available through the Library of Congress.
LC Card Number: 93-46145

Edited text and captions by Angela Royston, based on *Trees of North America* by Alan Mitchell.

Habitat paintings and headbands by Antonia Phillips. Identification and activities illustrations by Richard Coombes.

Editor   Diana Briscoe
Designer   James Lawrence
Design Assistant   Victoria Furbisher
Editorial Director Pippa Rubinstein

Printed in Spain

ISBN 1 85028 265 X

Contents

Trees Are Everywhere

There are trees everywhere, not just in woods and the countryside, but in town parks and gardens as well. In the countryside you are most likely to see native trees, those which grow naturally from their own seed and have grown here since the end of the last Ice Age 17,000 years ago.

You can see native trees in cities too, but they have usually been planted. Many other kinds of trees are planted as well. Most have been brought as seeds from other countries (introduced) and a few are crosses between different kinds of related trees.

The more you know about trees the more interesting they are. This book will help you recognize more than their leaves. In winter you can look at their bark and buds. In spring you can watch them flower and then produce seeds and fruits in summer and fall.

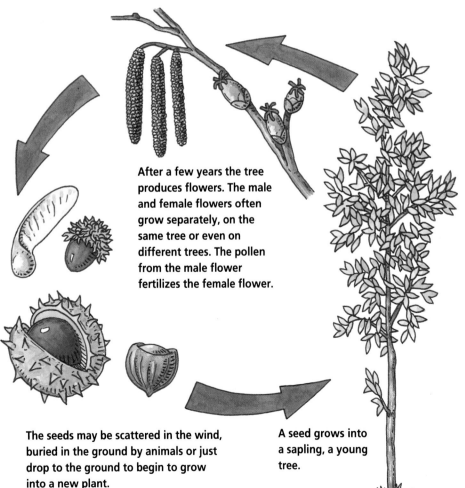

After a few years the tree produces flowers. The male and female flowers often grow separately, on the same tree or even on different trees. The pollen from the male flower fertilizes the female flower.

The seeds may be scattered in the wind, buried in the ground by animals or just drop to the ground to begin to grow into a new plant.

A seed grows into a sapling, a young tree.

The life of a tree

Some introduced trees become naturalized that is, they grow naturally from seed like native trees. A few introduced trees have to be grafted onto the stem of a native tree, but most are raised from seeds or cuttings, like the natives.

This mark on the trunk shows where one tree has been grafted or joined onto the stem of another. Grafting is necessary when a tree, like a Japanese Cherry, never produces a seed.

How to use this book

You can use this book to find out more about trees you can already recognize, and to identify a tree you do not know. To identify the two trees shown here, follow these steps.

Top-of-page Picture Bands

Each group of trees has a different picture band at the top of the page—they are shown below.

 **Broad-leaved Trees**

 **Ornamental Trees**

 **Evergreen Trees**

 **Conifers**

1 **Decide what kind of tree it is**—broadleaved, ornamental, evergreen, or coniferous. You will find descriptions of them at the start of each section. The tree below has broad, flat leaves so it will be in one of the first three sections. The tree on the left is coniferous, so turn to pages 58–77.

2 **Where is it growing?** If it is growing wild in the countryside it is most likely to be found in the first section. If it has obviously been planted for decoration, start looking in the second section. Only broadleaf trees that keep their leaves all winter are shown in the evergreen section.

3 **Check what shape the leaves are.** The conifer has single needles, so look through those trees, checking the shape of the tree, the flower and bark against those illustrated. You will find that the tree on the left is a Douglas Fir (see page 67).

4 **If you decide that the tree has been specially planted,** but you cannot find it in the second section, try the first section. Here the trees are arranged according to the shape of their leaves. The tree below has palmate leaves with five lobes. You will find it on page 23—it is a Norway Maple.

What To Look For

Parts of a Tree

When identifying a tree, it is important to check more than the shape of the leaves. Look at its general shape and the other parts of the tree shown here.

MALE FLOWERS: most trees rely on the wind to take their pollen to the female flower. Only those with scented blossom rely on insects.

FEMALE FLOWERS: their shape varies from one kind of tree to another. Some are so small they are hard to spot. Others are large and showy.

New BUDS form on the tree in late summer. They contain the leaves and flowers which will grow next spring. Look for the size and shape of buds.

FRUIT: Different kinds of broad-leaved trees produce different kinds of fruit to carry their seeds—berries, nuts, and seeds with wings are most common.

SHOOTS often sprout from the bottom of the trunk. They weaken the tree, but make the leaves easy to reach.

BARK is the outside layer of wood. What color is it—gray like beech, silver like birch or brown like spruce? Is it smooth, like beech, ridged like oak, stringy like redwood, or banded like cherry?

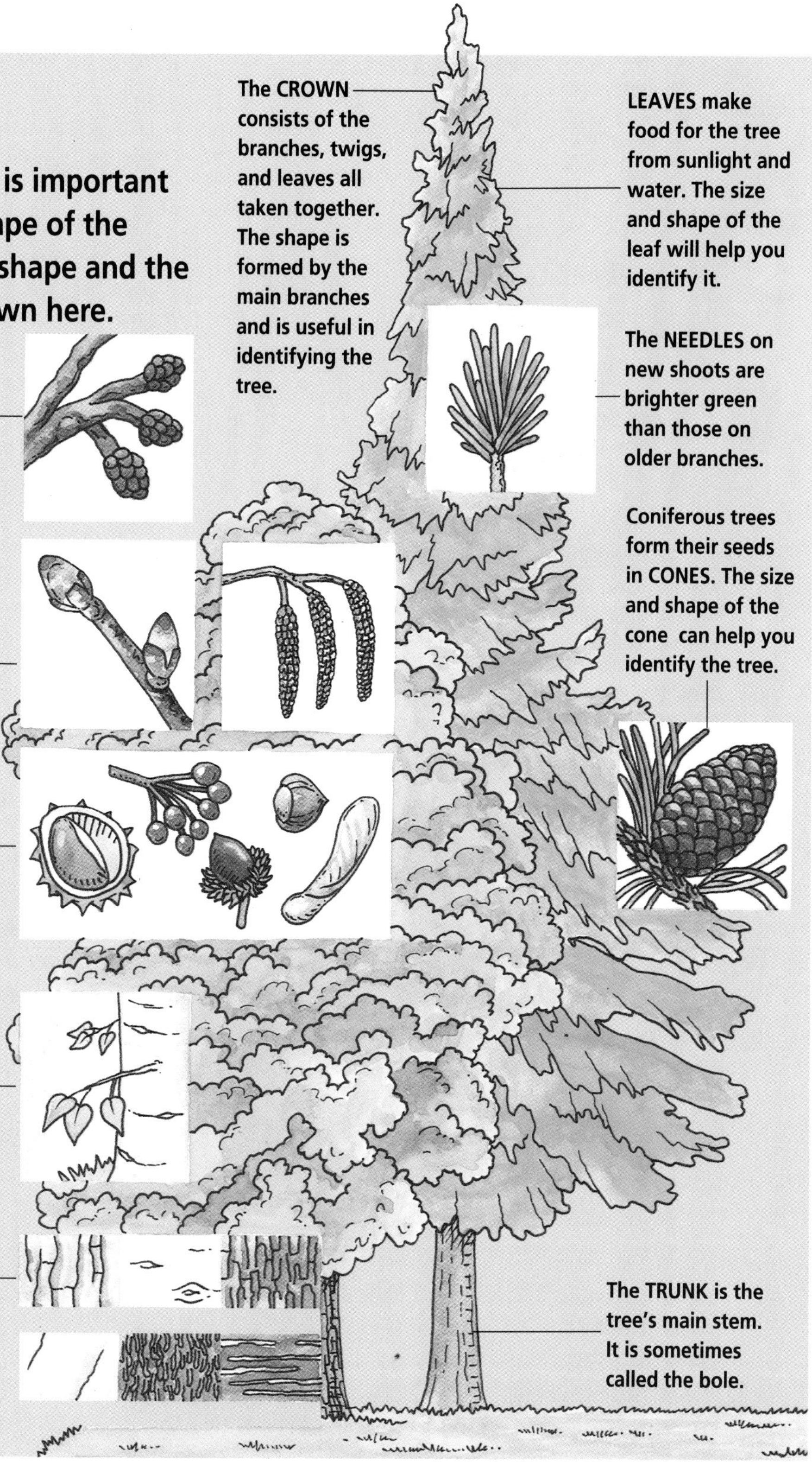

The CROWN consists of the branches, twigs, and leaves all taken together. The shape is formed by the main branches and is useful in identifying the tree.

LEAVES make food for the tree from sunlight and water. The size and shape of the leaf will help you identify it.

The NEEDLES on new shoots are brighter green than those on older branches.

Coniferous trees form their seeds in CONES. The size and shape of the cone can help you identify the tree.

The TRUNK is the tree's main stem. It is sometimes called the bole.

Shape of Trees

The overall shape of a tree is a useful clue to its identity. Here are some points to look for:

Many conifers are themselves cone-shaped, narrowing to a point at the top.

Some broad-leaved trees are also tall and narrow.

This tree has a spreading crown.

Do the branches arch downward like a basswood—or point upward like a maple?

Many trees have a weeping variety.

Shape of Leaves

When trying to identify a tree, the first thing to look at is the shape of its leaves.

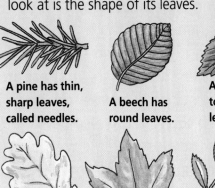

A pine has thin, sharp leaves, called needles.

A beech has round leaves.

A cherry has toothed, oval leaves.

An oak has lobed leaves.

A sycamore has palmate leaves.

A mountain ash has compound leaves made up of several leaflets.

Arrangement of Needles

Look at the way the needles of a coniferous tree grow—they are an important clue to identifying it.

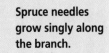

The leaves of a cypress enclose the branch like scales.

Spruce needles grow singly along the branch.

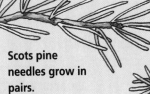

Scots pine needles grow in pairs.

Larch needles form rosettes.

Broad-leaved Deciduous Trees

Broad-leaved trees have broad, flat leaves. All the trees in the first part of this book are broad-leaved trees while those in the last section are conifers and have needles or scaly leaves. The trees in the first two sections are also deciduous. This means they lose their leaves in fall and survive the harsh winter weather with bare branches.

In North America, the greatest variety of broad-leaved trees grow in the East, particularly in Ontario, New England, around the Great Lakes, and in the southeastern US. Although the text tells you where you are most likely to see each tree, you may well see them in other areas too, especially in city parks, streets, or gardens.

Trees in this first section include all the large, common trees that you are likely to see growing in woods or the countryside. Most of them are native trees, that is, they have been growing and seeding themselves here for thousands of years. But not all common trees are native to the US. Some, like the Siberian Elm or Horse Chestnut, were introduced from other countries and now seed themselves like native trees.

All trees of the same kind are shown together. At first you will learn to recognize an oak tree or a birch tree. As you get better at telling one tree from another, you will be able to identify different types of oak or beech. The picture shows seven trees from this book. How many can you recognize?

Ash, Beech, Gray Birch, Washington Hawthorn, Horse Chestnut, Oak, Lombardy Poplar

Birch, Alder, & Beech

Alders and birches have simple, toothed leaves. Look at the bark to tell them apart.

Speckled Alder

Alders like wet ground so you are most likely to see Speckled Alders growing along the edges of lakes and streams, or in swampy ground. The bark is gray and smooth. Look for the tiny flowers in early spring before the leaves come out. The drooping catkins are male flowers. Female flowers are small cones, which become hard and black as they swell to about half an inch long during summer. Deer and moose may hide in thick clumps of alder. Watch too for birds feeding on the seeds.

Variation of European Gray Alder
Found across Canada and northeastern US
Grows up to 20 ft tall – Leaves 2–4 ins long

Paper Birch

You can tell a birch at once from its silvery-white bark and elegant shape. The Paper Birch gets its name from the bark, which peels off in papery strips to show the orange bark beneath. Look for the flowers in early spring. The yellowy catkins are male. The short, green catkins which grow just behind them are female flowers. In fall look for hanging cones of winged nutlets. The wood of the Paper Birch is made into ice cream sticks, toothpicks, broom handles, and toys. Native Americans used to make their canoes from it.

Native to Canada and northern US
Grows up to 70 ft tall
Leaves 2–4 ins long

Gray Birch

You are most likely to see Gray Birches growing along roadsides in woodland across eastern Canada and the northeastern US. It has long-tipped triangular leaves, which are smaller than those of the Paper Birch. Look too for the black, "Chinaman moustache" marks on the very white bark and the flexible, drooping branches.

Nova Scotia and Quebec to northern Virginia
Grows up to 30 ft tall
Leaves 2–3 ins long

Beeches have oval, toothed leaves. Lindens and Basswoods have heart-shaped, toothed leaves.

Littleleaf Linden

Lindens and basswoods belong to the same family and so have similar leaves and fruits. You can recognize the Littleleaf Linden from its small leaves and its starry, yellow flowers, which spread out rather than hang.

Introduced from Europe
Planted in many cities in southern Canada and northern and eastern US
Grows up to 70 ft tall
Leaves 2 ins long

Purple Beech

This beech is easy to recognize from its dark, purplish black leaves. In summer it gives good shade and produces beechnuts in fall like the American Beech. It is sometimes called Copper Beech.

Introduced from Europe
Planted in northeastern US and Pacific states
Grows up to 110 ft tall
Leaves 2–4 ins long

Basswood

Basswood is sometimes called the "Bee-tree," because it attracts so many bees when it flowers in early summer. The small, yellowy-white flowers hang in clusters and smell sweet. In autumn they turn into clusters of small, hard fruit. As the tree gets older the smooth, dark gray bark becomes ridged and scaly. The wood is soft and light, and is used to make food boxes and furniture.

Native to southern Canada and eastern US as far west as Oklahoma
Grows up to 100 ft tall
Leaves 3–6 ins long

American Beech

Even old beeches have smooth, light-gray bark. Look for the flowers just as the leaves are opening. The male flowers are round, yellowy balls that hang on slender stalks. The female flowers are much harder to spot. They are only a quarter of an inch long with hairy, red scales. By fall they have developed into shiny-brown beechnuts, protected in a prickly case. Squirrels, raccoons, bears, and game birds eat the nuts, and you can too.

Native to southeastern Canada and eastern US
Grows up to 130 ft tall
Leaves 2¼–5 ins long

Elms & Poplars

Elms have toothed, oval-shaped leaves. Three other trees from the elm family are shown on page 28.

Cedar Elm

Cedar Elms are the most common native elms in eastern Texas and the Southwest. They are often planted there to give shade. Their leaves are smaller than those of other elms, and are so thick and hard that they hardly bend in the wind. Instead each shoot of leaves moves as one rigid piece.

Native to extreme southwestern US
Grows up to 80 ft tall
Leaves 1–2 ins long

Slippery Elm

Slippery Elm gets its name from its sticky, aromatic inner bark which can be dried and made into cough medicine. To tell this elm from other elms try stroking its leaves. They should feel very rough. Look too at the bark. It is dark brown and deeply furrowed.

Native to southern Canada and eastern US
Grows up to 70 ft tall
Leaves 4–7 ins long

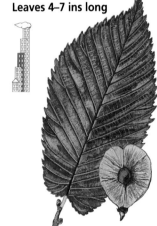

American Elm

You can recognize an American Elm from the shape of its broad, rounded crown. It is flat on top and the branches droop at the ends. Look too for the seeds which form in spring. They are flat and oval, and have a deep notch where the pointed wings meet. The wood is used for furniture and containers. American Elms used to be very common on lawns and city streets, but Dutch elm disease, spread by bark beetles, has killed many of them.

Native to central and eastern North America
Grows up to 100 ft tall
Leaves 3–6 ins long

These trees belong to the Poplars which are part of the willow family. They have triangular or rounded, toothed leaves.

Quaking Aspen

Quaking Aspens get their name from their leaves. Listen out for them as even the smallest breeze makes them flutter. In fall the trees look quite spectacular as the leaves turn a brilliant golden yellow. Look for signs of beavers, rabbits, and other animals who like to feed on the bark, leaves, and buds. You may even see a bear's scratch marks on the trunk.

Native in all North America from Labrador and Alaska, down Rocky Mountains to Mexico
Grows up to 70 ft tall
Leaves 1¼–3 ins long

Lombardy Poplar

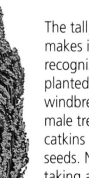

The tall, thin shape of this tree makes it one of the easiest to recognize. The trees are often planted in a line to form a windbreak. Lombardy Poplars are male trees. They have dark red catkins in early spring, but no seeds. New trees are produced by taking a cutting or root sprout from an existing tree.

Introduced from Europe
Planted throughout southern Canada and US
Grows up to 120 ft tall
Leaves 1½–3 ins long

Balsam Poplar

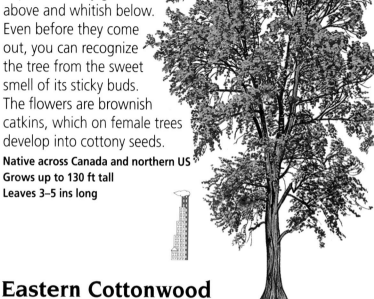

The leaves of the Balsam Poplar are shiny green above and whitish below. Even before they come out, you can recognize the tree from the sweet smell of its sticky buds. The flowers are brownish catkins, which on female trees develop into cottony seeds.

Native across Canada and northern US
Grows up to 130 ft tall
Leaves 3–5 ins long

Eastern Cottonwood

Cottonwoods get their name from the cottony, white seeds. Before the leaves open, look for the long, sticky buds and brown catkins. Male and female flowers look the same, but grow on separate trees. As the female flowers mature the seed capsules split. They give the tree another of its names, Necklace Poplar, because they look like strings of beads. When the capsules open, the tree releases masses of cotton, which blows everywhere.

Native throughout southern Canada, eastern, central US
Grows up to 100 ft tall
Leaves 3–7 ins long

Hornbeams & Willows

Hornbeams have toothed, simple leaves with deep veins. They are similar to birch and beech, but are duller green.

European Hornbeam

Although the American Hornbeam looks more spectacular in fall, the European Hornbeam is usually planted in parks and gardens instead of it. The kind you are most likely to see is Pyramidal Hornbeam, so called for its rounded, egg shape. In winter look for the long, slim buds.

Introduced from Europe
Planted for ornament, mainly in the East
Grows up to 60 ft tall
Leaves 3–4³/₄ ins long

Hophornbeam

This tree takes its name from the clusters of fruit which look rather like the hops with which beer is flavored. They are white in summer, but turn brown and stay on the tree all winter. They are a good way of identifying the tree. Look closely at the cone-like clusters. Each brown nutlet is held in a papery, light-brown sac. The tree is sometimes called Ironwood, after its tough, hard wood, which is used for tool handles and fence posts.

Native to southeastern Canada and eastern US
Grows up to 50 ft tall
Leaves 2–5 ins long

American Hornbeam

The American Hornbeam is sometimes called Blue-beech or Water-beech, because the leaves and blue-gray bark look like those of beech. They are much smaller than beech trees, however, and often grow only as a shrub. In fall its leaves turn orange and red. Clusters of tiny, green nutlets held in three-pointed scales develop in late summer. The wood is very tough and hard, and is used for tool handles and other small items. Watch for deer feeding on the twigs and bark, and for grouse eating the nutlets.

Native to southeastern Canada and eastern US
Grows up to 30 ft tall
Leaves 2–4¹/₂ ins long

Willows have long, thin leaves which are green above and paler or whitish below. The best way to tell them apart is by the shape of the tree.

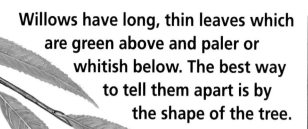

Coastal Plain Willow

This small tree often grows only as a shrub. Its branches spread or slightly droop. Look for it alongside streams and swamps across the Coastal Plain. Notice how hairy the leaves are when they first open.

Native to southeastern US
Grows up to 30 ft tall – Leaves 2–4 ins long

Black Willow

This willow grows very large and has two or three blackish trunks and upright branches. They grow in wet soil and are often planted alongside streams and rivers to stop the banks eroding and so prevent flooding. Like other willows, the flowers are long, yellow or green catkins. The wood is used for furniture, doors, toys, and boxes. In the past it was made into charcoal for gunpowder.

Native to eastern and southern US
Grows up to 100 ft tall
Leaves 3–5 ins long

Babylon Weeping Willow

You will see this weeping willow planted in parks, gardens, and cemeteries, especially near water. New twigs are yellowish green and hang straight down. By winter they have turned olive-brown. It is one of the first willows to come into leaf and among the last to shed its leaves.

Introduced from China
Planted on East Coast and west to Missouri, and on West Coast
Grows up to 40 ft tall
Leaves 2¹/₂–5 ins long

Peachleaf Willow

The Peachleaf Willow is smaller than the Black Willow, and its leaves are shorter and wider. It is common on the northern plains where it is planted along riverbanks to prevent erosion.

Native to southern Canada, northern US, and plains
Grows up to 60 ft tall
Leaves 2–4¹/₂ ins long

Oaks

The best way to recognize an oak tree is by its acorns and leaves. There are several groups of oaks. White Oaks have deeply lobed leaves. Red Oaks have pointed and deeply-lobed leaves. The leaves of Willow Oaks and Live Oaks have few or no lobes.

Post Oak

The best way to identify a Post Oak is from its leaves. The two middle lobes are larger than the rest, so the whole leaf is shaped a bit like a cross. As its name suggests, the wood is used for posts, railroad crossties, and in buildings.

Native to southern and eastern US
Grows up to 70 ft tall
Leaves 3–6 ins long

Bur Oak

This White Oak gets its name from the hairy, scaly cup which holds its acorns – up to 2 inches long, longer than any other native oak. The leaves are also the biggest.

Native to southern Canada, Midwest, and down Mississippi River to Gulf of Mexico
Grows up to 80 ft tall
Leaves 4–10 ins long

Pin Oak

Pin Oaks are the most common tree in Central Park, New York, and in many city streets in the East and west. You can tell a Pin Oak from its slender, pin-like twigs and the tufts of hairs on the undersides of the shiny, dark green leaves. Look too at the acorns. They are nearly round and held in a thin, saucer-shaped cup.

Native from Midwest to East Coast
Grows up to 90 ft tall – Leaves 3–5 ins long

White Oak

This tree is the most common member of the White Oak group. The leaves are reddish when they first open, then turn bright green above and whitish below. They turn red or brown in fall and often remain on the tree. Look for the dangling, male catkins in spring. The female flowers develop into acorns, which provide food for birds, squirrels, and other animals. Notice how shallow the acorn cup is. White Oaks have sturdy trunks and wide, spreading branches. The colonists used them for building ships. Their wood is still important and is used for making barrels for whiskey.

Native to southeastern Canada and eastern US
Grows up to 100 ft tall
Leaves 4–9 ins long

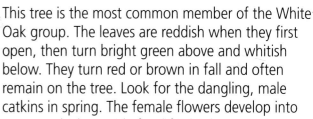

Willow Oak

This tree gets its name from its leaves, which look a bit like those of a willow tree (see page 15). The leaves are yellow at first, then turn from green to golden in fall. The slender branches give plenty of shade, and you will often see them in city streets. Look for squirrels and birds feeding on the acorns.

Native to southern US States and north along East Coast to New Jersey
Grows up to 120 ft tall – Leaves 2–4½ ins long

Chestnut Oak

Chestnut Oaks get their name from their leaves, which look a bit like those of the American Chestnut (see page 21). They have shallower lobes than the white oaks. The acorns are a rich red-brown. The gray bark becomes thick and ridged and full of tannin. It used to be used for tanning leather.

Native to New England and eastern US
Up to 80 ft tall – Leaves 4–8 ins long

Red Oak

Red Oaks are named from their fall colors. Although they are dull green in spring and summer, they turn dark red or brown in fall. Scarlet Oaks turn even redder, but are less common. You can see acorns on Red Oaks at all times. They are small and take two years to develop. The tree has stout, spreading branches. The wood is strong and is used for mine supports and railroad crossties, as well as for furniture and flooring.

Native to southern Canada and eastern US
Grows up to 130 ft tall
Leaves 4–9 ins long

Live Oak

Live Oaks are so called because they are evergreen. The thick, oval leaves sometimes have a pointed tip. You are most likely to see them growing in sandy soils, including dunes and marshes. Look for clumps of Spanish moss hanging from them. Different varieties of Live Oak grow in Arizona and California, in the Sierra Nevada and the Coast Range mountains.

Native to Gulf Coast and East Coast as far north as Virginia
Grows up to 50 ft tall
Leaves 1½–4 ins long

How A Tree Grows

Trees never stop growing. Every year new shoots grow at the ends of the branches making the crown wider and taller. And every year a new layer of wood forms under the bark making the trunk and branches a little thicker.

Estimating the height

1 **Take 29 equal paces away from the tree**. Ask a friend to hold a stick upright at that point.
2 **Walk another pace away from the tree.** Crouch or lie down so that your eye is as low as the ground.
3 **Look past the stick to the top of the tree.** Ask your friend to raise or lower their hand on the stick until the bottom of their hand lines up with the tree's top.
4 **Measure the distance from their hand to the ground** and multiply it by ten to give you the rough height of the tree.

Inside the trunk

When a tree has been blown over or chopped down, have a look at the pattern of rings left on the stump. They can tell you the whole history of the tree, because each ring represents the layer of wood formed in one year of the tree's life.

1 **Count the rings to find out how old the tree was.**
2 **Look for rings which are particularly wide or narrow.** Wide rings show years when the tree had plenty of rain and grew well. Narrow rings show years of drought (little rain) or cold weather when the tree grew only a little.
3 **If the rings are closer together on one side than the other,** try to work out why the tree grew less on the crowded side. Is there a wall or another tree close by?

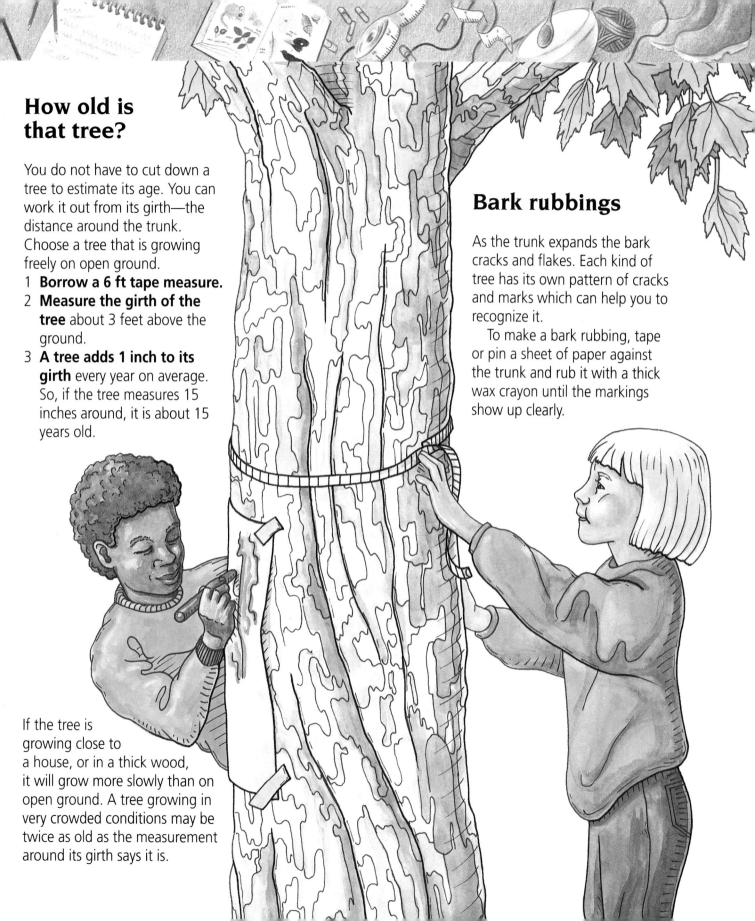

How old is that tree?

You do not have to cut down a tree to estimate its age. You can work it out from its girth—the distance around the trunk. Choose a tree that is growing freely on open ground.

1 **Borrow a 6 ft tape measure.**
2 **Measure the girth of the tree** about 3 feet above the ground.
3 **A tree adds 1 inch to its girth** every year on average. So, if the tree measures 15 inches around, it is about 15 years old.

If the tree is growing close to a house, or in a thick wood, it will grow more slowly than on open ground. A tree growing in very crowded conditions may be twice as old as the measurement around its girth says it is.

Bark rubbings

As the trunk expands the bark cracks and flakes. Each kind of tree has its own pattern of cracks and marks which can help you to recognize it.

To make a bark rubbing, tape or pin a sheet of paper against the trunk and rub it with a thick wax crayon until the markings show up clearly.

Hawthorns & Sycamores

You can tell Hawthorns by their jagged, toothed leaves and spiky thorns.

Washington Hawthorn

This hawthorn is one on the showiest and most attractive hawthorns, and is often planted in cities in the East. It flowers in late spring. In fall the leaves turn scarlet and orange before dropping. The shiny-red berries, however, stay on the tree all winter.

Native to southeastern US and north along the coast to Massachusetts
Grows up to 30 ft tall
Leaves 1½–2½ ins long

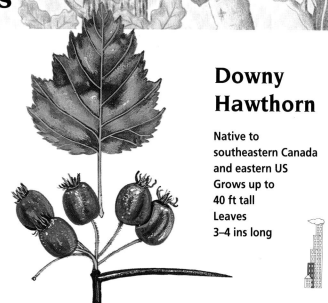

Downy Hawthorn

Native to southeastern Canada and eastern US
Grows up to 40 ft tall
Leaves 3–4 ins long

The young leaves of Downy Hawthorn are covered with white hair, and so are the young twigs and fruit as well. The flowers are larger than other hawthorns and grow into drooping clusters of dark red berries with black spots. Some Downy Hawthorns have thorns up to 3 inches long, while others have almost no thorns at all.

Scarlet Hawthorn

You cannot miss hawthorns in the spring when they are covered with white flowers. Scarlet Hawthorn grows into a small, sturdy tree and is named for its red berries. You can tell them from other bright red-berried hawthorns by the dark spots on them. Black Hawthorn has similar leaves, but black berries. It grows mainly in the west.

Native from Iowa and Minnesota east to Canadian and US coasts
Grows up to 20 ft tall – Leaves 2–4 ins long

Sycamores and London Planes have large leaves with five lobes, rather like the five fingers of a hand. Chestnuts have long, narrow, toothed leaves.

London Plane

This tree has been planted in cities from coast to coast. It stands up well to pollution and to having its roots below concrete. You can tell it from a sycamore because its leaves have deeper lobes, its bark is brown and yellow, and it has four to six fruits on each stalk. Be careful not to confuse its leaves with those of maples

Hybrid between Sycamore and Oriental Plane
Planted across US – Up to 100 ft tall – Leaves 5–10 ins long

Sycamore

Sycamores can grow very tall with a big, straight trunk. Some trunks measure more than 10 feet across. The bark is blue-white and peels off the trunk in large flakes, leaving brown, gray, and green patches. On very large trunks, the bark is dark brown and furrowed into deep, scaly ridges. The wood is used for furniture and flooring. The tiny green flowers turn into brown balls, which hang down on long stalks. The California Sycamore has five small balls strung along each stalk.

Native to eastern US
Grows up to 100 ft tall – Leaves 4–8 ins long

American Chestnut

You can recognize a Sweet Chestnut from its long, toothed leaves and from its fruit. Look for the spiny burs which split open to release two or three shiny brown chestnuts. American Chestnuts are more like shrubs than trees, though sometimes they grow to a good height. They have been virtually wiped out in many parts of the US by Chestnut Blight. Hybrids of Chinese and American trees, however, resist the disease and are being developed to replace them.

Native to eastern and southeastern US
Grows up to 20 ft tall, rarely 60 ft
Leaves 5–9 ins long

Maples

All maples have pairs of leaves, mostly with 3- or 5-pointed lobes. The middle lobe is sometimes divided into farther lobes.

Silver Maple

Silver Maples get their name from the silvery underside of their leaves. When the wind blows, the leaves seem to turn silver. Even when the leaves turn yellow or red in fall, the underside remains silver. The smooth bark is silvery-gray. Clusters of deep-red flowers open in early spring before the leaves. Pairs of winged seedš form in early summer and are scattered by the wind.

Native across eastern North America south of Quebec
Grows up to 120 ft tall – Leaves 4–6 ins long

Sugar Maple

The leaves of the Sugar Maple turn the brightest reds, oranges, and yellow of all the maples in fall. To tell this tree from other similar maples, look at the fruit. The angle between the wings in each pair of seeds is more acute than in some maples. The wood is used for furniture, flooring, and boxes, and for putting a thin layer, or veneer, over other woods. Each tree can give up to 60 gallons of sap each year. This can be made into maple sugar and syrup.

Native across eastern North America, but not southeastern US
Grows up to 100 ft tall
Leaves 3$\frac{1}{2}$–5$\frac{1}{2}$ ins long

Red Maple

In fall the Red Maple has red seeds and leaves. In spring look for its red flowers and shoots. The underside of the leaves is silvery, like the Silver Maple, but the leaves are smaller and are not so deeply lobed. The red maple leaf is Canada's national emblem.

Native across eastern and southern US
Grows up to 90 ft tall
Leaves 2$\frac{1}{2}$–4 ins long

Box Elder

Although Box Elder is a maple, its leaves are more like an ash than a maple. However, its pairs of winged seeds confirm that it is a maple. Many hang on the tree right through winter. You will see it growing in waste places and by roadsides, as well as along streams and moist valleys.

Native to Alberta and eastern US, and scattered across the interior to California
Grows up to 60 ft tall
Leaves 6 ins long

Rocky Mountain Maple

This low, bushy tree is the common small maple of the western mountains.

**Native to the Rocky Mountains from Alaska to Arizona
Grows up to 30 ft tall
Leaves 3–6 ins long**

Planetree Maple

This maple grows well in poor soils, sea winds, and polluted cities. The leaves, however, are not as spectacular in fall as many of our native maples. They have shallow lobes and toothed, wavy edges.

**Introduced from Europe – Planted across US
Grows up to 70 ft tall – Leaves 3¹⁄₂–6 ins long**

Norway Maple

This tree is similar to the Sugar Maple and they are often planted together in streets. You can tell them apart by their bark. The Norway Maple's bark is smooth with shallow, narrow ridges, while the Sugar Maple's bark is lighter and scaly with deep ridges. The tree is at its best in spring, when the yellow flowers open before the leaves, and in fall, when the leaves turn deep yellow.

**Introduced from northern and central Europe
Planted across US and southern Canada
Grows up to 80 ft tall
Leaves 4–7 ins long**

Buckeyes & Ashes

Buckeyes and Horse Chestnuts have large, palmate leaves with five to seven leaflets. The best way to tell them apart is by their fruit.

Horse Chestnut

It is hard to miss this tree in spring when it is covered with big, white, candle-like flowers. By fall the flowers have turned into shiny-brown nuts in spiky cases. Unlike Sweet Chestnuts, the nuts of the Horse Chestnut are poisonous. It is said that in Turkey they were used to make a cough medicine for horses, and so the tree got its name. Look for the large, sticky buds in early spring. They are good way to tell the tree from the American Buckeyes.

Introduced from southeastern Europe
Widely planted in streets and parks
across US and southern Canada
Grows up to 70 ft tall
Leaves 3–7 ins long

Yellow Buckeye

You can tell Buckeyes from Horse Chestnuts by looking at the leaves. Horse Chestnut leaflets have no stalks of their own, while Buckeye leaflets join at the end of short stalks. In fall the leaves turn brilliant orange. The flowers are yellow and the nuts are held in a smooth, or slightly pitted, case.

Native to north
eastern US,
south of New England
Grows up to
90 ft tall
Leaves
3½–7 ins long

Ohio Buckeye

This is the state tree of Ohio. You can easily tell it from other buckeyes by crushing one of the leaves or twigs. If it smells unpleasant, then it is Ohio Buckeye. The nuts are held in spiny cases. Early pioneers used to carry a buckeye seed in their pocket to keep away rheumatism.

Native from Pennsylvania
to Oklahoma
Grows up to 70 ft tall
Leaves 2–6 ins long

You can recognize ash trees by their leaves, which are divided into many pairs of leaflets with a single leaflet at the tip, and by the bunches of long-winged seeds.

Black Ash

Black Ash grows mainly in the North. Look for it in wet, swampy soils and in forests of coniferous and broad-leaved trees. To tell it from other ashes, rub the gray bark. If the soft, scaly plates rub off easily, it is Black Ash. It gets its name from the dark brown inner wood, which is split into strips and made into baskets and barrel hoops. So, not surprisingly, it is also known as Basket Ash and Hoop Ash.

Native to eastern Canada and northeastern US
Grows up to 50 ft tall – Leaves 12–16 ins long

Native of southern Canada and US east of Rocky Mountains Grows up to 60 ft tall in northern areas Leaves 6–10 ins long

Green Ash

Green Ash is the most widespread ash tree, but it is not as common as White Ash. You can tell them apart by their leaves. Those of Green Ash are shiny green above, and paler and slightly hairy beneath, while those of the white ash are dark green above, and whitish and sometimes hairy below. The flowers are greenish and, like most ash trees, have no petals.

White Ash

White Ash is the commonest eastern ash. You will find it growing wild along streams and in woods, or planted in city parks. The purple flowers do not have any petals. Look for them in spring before the leaves come out. Male and female flowers grow on separate trees. In fall the clusters of long-winged seeds hang from the female trees. The wood of White Ash is used for making baseball bats, tennis rackets, hockey sticks, and other sports equipment.

Native to eastern North America
Grows up to 130 ft tall – Leaves 8–12 ins long

Oregon Ash

This is the only big-leaved native ash tree in the west. It has very large leaves, which are often over a foot long, on hairy shoots.

Native to west coast US
Grows up to 80 ft tall
Leaves 6–14 ins long

Walnuts & Hickories

Hickories belong to the walnut family. Their leaves have many paired leaflets, like those of ash trees. You can tell them from ash trees because they produce nuts rather than winged seeds.

Pecan

Pecans and Black Walnuts are often planted together. It is easy to tell the older trees apart because the bark of Pecans grows paler and flaky, while that of Black Walnut becomes black and more ridged. You can eat the bright pink nuts. They are oblong and covered with a thin, dark brown shell.

Native to Mississippi Valley Planted across eastern US and commercially in southern US
Grows up to 130 ft tall
Leaves 12–20 ins long

Black Walnut

The Black Walnut has long, shiny, bright green leaves with numerous leaflets, which are often without a single one at the end. The bark is dark brown with deep, scaly ridges. The wood is valuable for making furniture and gunstocks. The nuts are hidden inside a hard, thick shell, with a thick, green, outer husk. You must pick the nuts early, however, because squirrels and other animals like to eat them too.

Native to eastern US to the Canadian border
Grows up to 90 ft tall – Leaves 12–24 ins long

Bitternut Hickory

This is the hickory found most frequently in the Appalachian woods. You can recognize it from the small, bright yellow buds in winter. If in doubt, try tasting the nuts. They are much too bitter even for animals to eat, although a few rabbits have been seen to nibble them.

Native to eastern US north to Quebec
Grows up to 80 ft tall
Leaves 6–10 ins long

Shagbark Hickory

This tree is named after its rough, shaggy bark. It begins to flake into long, curly strips when the tree is about 25 years old. The bark of Shellbark Hickory is similar, but Shellbark leaves have seven leaflets rather than five. The name hickory comes from the Native American word *pawcohiccora*—the oily food which they made after soaking the nuts in boiling water.

Native to eastern US and southeastern Canada
Grows up to 100 ft tall
Leaves 8–14 ins long

Mockernut Hickory

The leaves of Mockernut Hickory have seven pairs of leaflets like several other hickories. The best way to recognize them is from the strong, grassy smell you get when you crush a leaf, and by the dense hairs which cover the undersides of the leaves. You can eat the round nuts, but you must collect them early before the squirrels and other animals beat you to it. Hickory wood is used for furniture, flooring, baseball bats, and skis.

Native to eastern US
Grows up to 80 ft tall
Leaves 8–20 ins long

Pignut Hickory

Pignut Hickory is sometimes called Smoothbark Hickory after its smooth, light-gray bark. It is one of the most common hickories in the southern Appalachians. Its leaves usually have only five leaflets and its nuts open later than others. The husk splits right back to the base and the small, smooth nuts may be sweet or bitter.

Native to southeastern Canada and eastern US
Grows up to 120 ft tall
Leaves 6–10 ins long

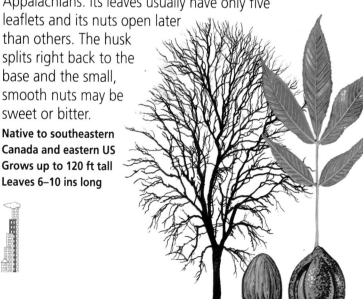

Other Broad-leaved Trees

Hackberry, Sugarberry, and Keaki all belong to the elm family. Their toothed, oval leaves end in a long point. You can tell them apart by their fruit.

Sugarberry

Sugarberries are small-leaved Hackberries, but their berries are orange-red in color. Watch for robins, mockingbirds, and other songbirds feeding on them. Although this tree can grow very tall, it may be kept small or cut back to form hedges.

Native to southeastern US
Grows up to 80 ft tall
Leaves 2¹⁄₂–4 ins long

Hackberry

The leaves of Hackberries are similar to those of elms (see page 12), but the fruit is quite different. Instead of winged nutlets, Hackberries have dark purple berries. Watch for woodpeckers, pheasants, and other birds feeding on these sweetish berries. Mites and fungi also like Hackberries. They produce the deformed bushy growths in the branches, known as "witches'-brooms."

Native to Midwest and
northeastern US north
to Quebec
Grows up to 90 ft tall
Leaves 2–5 ins long

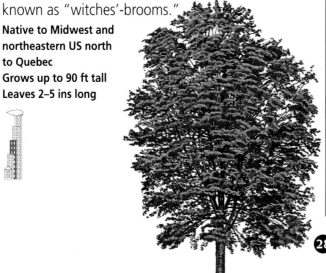

Keaki

This tree is particularly attractive in fall when the green leaves turn yellow, pink, and amber. It is resistant to Dutch elm disease and so makes a good substitute for American Elms. In Japan the wood is used for making furniture, lacquered boxes, and trays.

Introduced from Japan
Planted widely in streets and parks
Grows up to 70 ft tall – Leaves 1–3¹⁄₂ ins long

Sassafras and Sweetgum both have aromatic bark. Tree of Heaven, Honeylocust, and Kentucky Coffeetree have many pairs of small leaflets.

Sassafras

The leaves of Sassafras vary in shape. Some are oval, others are shaped like mittens, and some have three lobes. All have dark blue berries growing on bright red stalks. When the Europeans first came to America, they thought the aromatic root bark would cure all diseases and shipped it back to Europe. Today the oil is used to perfume soap, and to flavor root beer.

Native to southern and
eastern US
Grows up to 60 ft tall
Leaves 3–5 ins long

Sweetgum

Sweetgum leaves look rather like maple leaves (see page 22) and, like them, they turn scarlet in fall. But if you crush a leaf you will know at once that this is a Sweetgum by the strong, sweet, aromatic smell. Look too for drooping, prickly, brown fruits. Resin is collected from under the bark and is used in medicines and chewing gum.

Native to eastern and southeastern US
Grows up to 100 ft tall
Leaves 3–6 ins long

Kentucky Coffeetree

You can tell this tree from others by its enormous leaves, up to 30 inches long, which are, made up of many leaflets. The dark brown pods each contain several black beans which used to be roasted and used as a substitute for coffee. That was how it got its name. Be careful, though, as the raw seeds are poisonous.

Native to Midwest – Planted widely in parks and yards
Grows up to 70 ft tall – Leaves 12–36 ins long

Tree of Heaven

This tree has been planted in nearly every city in North America. The leaves are deep-red when they first open, then change to green. Notice the two large teeth, or small lobes, near the stalk. They are a good way of telling them from other, similar, leaves. The clusters of yellow, male flowers smell unpleasant and some people are allergic to their pollen.

Introduced from China
Grows right across temperate North America
Grows up to 80 ft tall
Leaves 12–14 ins long

Honeylocust

The trunk and branches of most wild Honeylocusts are covered with groups of sharp spines, but a variety without spines is usually planted in towns. The tree is a good one for attracting wildlife. They like to feed on the sweet pulp of its long, thin pods.

Native to Midwest, and south to Gulf of Mexico
Planted very widely in cities
Grows up to 80 ft tall
Leaves 4–8 ins long

Leaves

Leaves are the tree's food factories. While they are making food for the tree, they give off oxygen, which is what we all breathe. So, without plants and trees, all living creatures would die.

Leaves are green because they contain a pigment called **chlorophyll**. This traps the energy of sunlight to make sugar from water from the soil and carbon dioxide, which the tree collects from the air. This sugar dissolves in more water to become sap, the tree's food, which is taken down thin tubes (veins) to the roots where it is stored. During this process, called **photosynthesis**, the tree releases oxygen back into the air.

Leaf skeletons

You can see the veins in a leaf most clearly when the rest of the leaf has gone. Sycamore leaves are good ones to use.

1. **Boil 2 pints (5 cups) of water in a large pan** and add 1 tablespoon of borax (washing soda). Ask an adult to help you with this.
2. **Drop the leaves into the pan** and leave them to simmer for half an hour.
3. **When the pan has cooled,** drain and rinse the leaves in cold water and leave to dry.
4. **Use an old toothbrush** to carefully brush away all of the leaf except the veins.

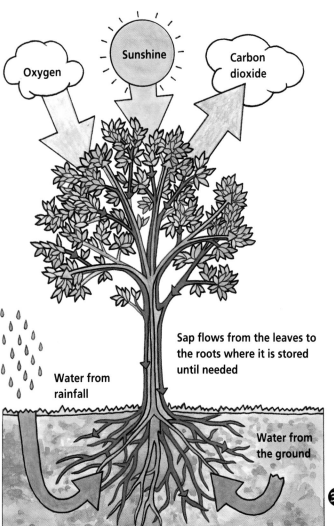

Oxygen

Sunshine

Carbon dioxide

Sap flows from the leaves to the roots where it is stored until needed

Water from rainfall

Water from the ground

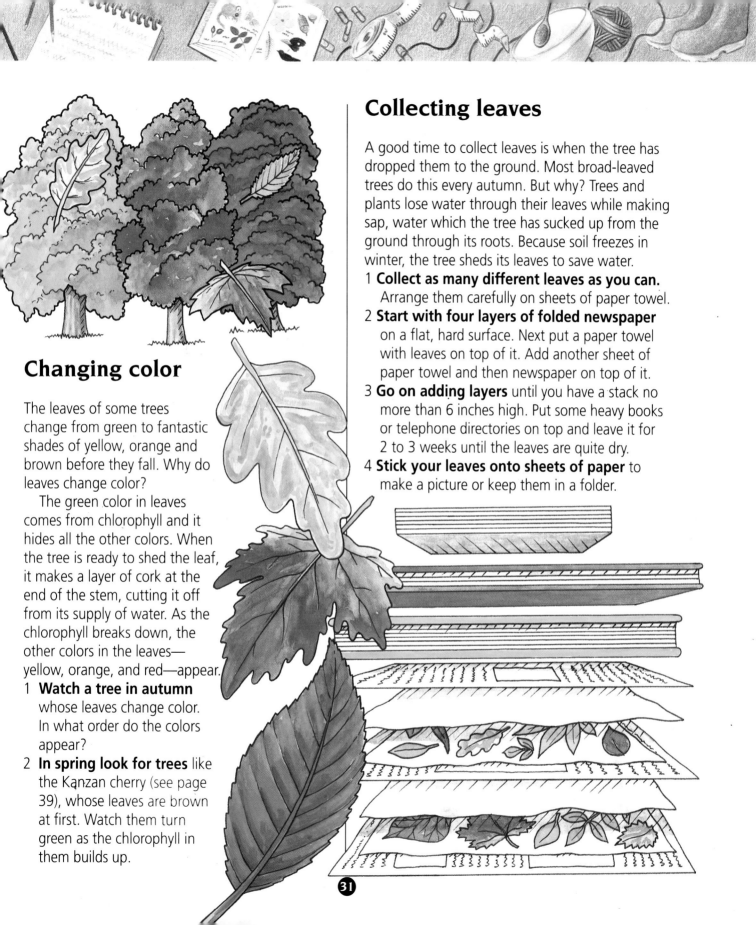

Collecting leaves

A good time to collect leaves is when the tree has dropped them to the ground. Most broad-leaved trees do this every autumn. But why? Trees and plants lose water through their leaves while making sap, water which the tree has sucked up from the ground through its roots. Because soil freezes in winter, the tree sheds its leaves to save water.

1 **Collect as many different leaves as you can.** Arrange them carefully on sheets of paper towel.
2 **Start with four layers of folded newspaper** on a flat, hard surface. Next put a paper towel with leaves on top of it. Add another sheet of paper towel and then newspaper on top of it.
3 **Go on adding layers** until you have a stack no more than 6 inches high. Put some heavy books or telephone directories on top and leave it for 2 to 3 weeks until the leaves are quite dry.
4 **Stick your leaves onto sheets of paper** to make a picture or keep them in a folder.

Changing color

The leaves of some trees change from green to fantastic shades of yellow, orange and brown before they fall. Why do leaves change color?

The green color in leaves comes from chlorophyll and it hides all the other colors. When the tree is ready to shed the leaf, it makes a layer of cork at the end of the stem, cutting it off from its supply of water. As the chlorophyll breaks down, the other colors in the leaves—yellow, orange, and red—appear.

1 **Watch a tree in autumn** whose leaves change color. In what order do the colors appear?
2 **In spring look for trees** like the Kanzan cherry (see page 39), whose leaves are brown at first. Watch them turn green as the chlorophyll in them builds up.

Ornamental Trees

Many of the trees planted in streets, parks, and yards have been introduced from countries as far away as Japan, China, and India. Many of them are small trees, but all of them have been planted because they are particularly decorative in some way.

Although a few ornamental trees are fruit trees, only the trees on the first two pages produce fruits you can eat. The others are planted for their beautiful blossoms, or because their fruits look attractive. The apples and cherries are mostly too sour for us to eat, but birds, squirrels, and other animals feed on them.

Other trees, such as magnolias, are planted just for their big, showy flowers. It is easy to recognize them when the flowers are out, but try to spot them at other times of the year too. Look closely at their leaves, bark, and seeds.

Not all the trees in this section have been introduced from Europe or Asia. Eastern Redbud and many other trees are natives, and you may see them growing wild in the countryside as well as in cities. Similarly, do not assume that only ornamental trees are specially planted. You will also see many ornamental evergreens and conifers in streets and gardens. The picture shows eight trees from this book. How many can you recognize?

Japanese Cherries: "Kwanzan," "Shimidsu," Japanese Crab Apple, Honeylocust (p.29), American Mountain Ash, White Oak (p.16), Pear, Pissard's Purple Plum.

Fruit Trees

In the right climate these trees will all produce fruit that you can eat.

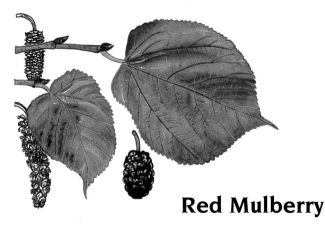

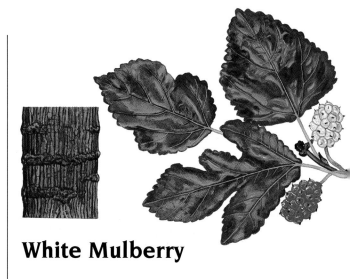

Red Mulberry

You will see Red Mulberry growing wild in woods as well as in yards and on roadsides. The toothed leaves are mainly oval , but on young twigs they may have two or three lobes. By late spring the long, narrow clusters of flowers have developed into dark purple or red berries. Both people and animals, especially songbirds, like to eat the berries. The bark is brown and scaly. The wood is used for furniture, fence posts, and farm tools.

Native to southeastern Canada and eastern US
Grows up to 60 ft tall – Leaves 4–7 ins long

White Mulberry

You can tell White Mulberry from other mulberries by its shiny leaves. They are smooth on top, but slightly hairy below. The fruits may be pink, purple, or white. Both birds and people like to eat them. Like other mulberries, they are made up of many tiny, bead-like berries, clustered together. In late spring you will find the sidewalks littered with them. In China the leaves are the main food for silkworms, but when silk farmers introduced the tree to the southeastern US, they did not succeed in producing silk.

Introduced from China – Planted across US and now grows wild in East and West Coast states
Grows up to 40 ft tall – Leaves 2¹/₂–7 ins long

Fig

Fig trees are easy to recognize from their large, leathery leaves, which are deeply cut into three or five lobes. They are grown for their juicy fruits, which take two years to ripen from green to black.

Introduced from Western Asia
Planted on West and South Coasts
Grows up to 30 ft tall
Leaves up to 12 ins long

Common Persimmon

In Arkansas and Oklahoma you are most likely to see Persimmons growing in hedges for miles along the road. In other places it grows in woods and clearings near a tall tree. The yellowy-white flowers open in July and develop into orange or purple-brown berries. They are very tart at first, but when they have fully ripened they are sweet enough to eat and taste rather like dates. Opossums, raccoons, skunks, deer, and birds like to eat these berries. The wood is used to make the heads of golf-clubs and as a veneer for furniture.

Native to southeastern US
Grows up to 70 ft tall
Leaves 2¹/₂–6 ins long

Loquat

Loquats can only produce fruit in the warmest states. The long, toothed leaves stay on the tree all year round. Look for it in courtyards, small gardens, and on walls. The flowers open in late summer, and will only survive the winter if there is no frost. In spring they ripen into round, orange fruits.

Introduced from China and Japan
Grown in California and in southern states
Grows up to 30 ft tall
Leaves up to 12 ins long

Peach

Peach trees are grown mainly in orchards for their juicy fruit. But some now grow wild in hedges by the side of the road. Look for their long, thin leaves and pink flowers, which look like pale roses.

Introduced from China
Grown in the South & California
Grows up to 24 ft tall
Leaves up to 7 ins long

Crab Apples & Pear

These fruit trees are planted because of their attractive blossom and fruit. Only the Sweet Crab Apple and Pear fruits are sweet enough for people to eat.

Pillar Apple

You are most likely to see this tree planted in streets and narrow plazas. It does not spread widely and produces only a few, small, yellow or red apples. In fall the leaves turn brilliant colors. It is also known as the Tschonoski Crab.

Introduced from Japan
Grows up to 45 ft tall
Leaves up to 5 ins long

Sweet Crab Apple

This tree grows wild by streams and woods. Crab Apples belong to the rose family and their flowers look like those of wild roses. In parks and gardens you will often see a variety called "Charlottae," which has double flowers. The tiny, yellow-green apples ripen in late summer. They are sour to eat, but are often made into preserves and cider.

Native from Illinois, South Ontario, and New York south to Arkansas and Georgia
Grows up to 30 ft tall
Leaves 2–4 ins long

Prairie Crab Apple

As its name suggests, you will find this tree growing wild alongside streams in the prairies. Look for birds, squirrels, rabbits, and other animals feeding on the small, yellow-green apples. The variety called Bechtel's Crab is often planted in gardens. It has so many double, pink flowers it looks more like a Japanese cherry tree in blossom than an apple tree.

Native to eastern US prairies and upper Mississippi Valley
Grows up to 30 ft tall
Leaves 2$\frac{1}{2}$–4 ins long

Common Pear

You can eat the fruit which grows on this pear tree. Look for the white flowers in spring. Pear trees live for many years. Their wood is very strong and was used by the French to make dressers and other furniture.

Introduced from Europe and western Asia
Grows wild in eastern and northwestern US
Grows up to 40 ft tall
Leaves 1¹/₂–3 ins long

Japanese Crab Apple

This tree has been planted in many town gardens. It is at its best in May, when you can see both the bright red buds and the pink and white flowers. The tiny, yellow fruits form only every few years.

Introduced from Japan
Planted in Ontario south to Delaware and in California
Grows up to 30 ft tall
Leaves 1¹/₂–3¹/₂ ins long

Purple Crab Apple

The Purple Crab Apple is well named because it has purplish flowers and dark red fruit no more than 1 inch long. When the leaves first open they are purplish red, but soon turn glossy green.

Hybrid – Introduced from
France and bred in Canada,
Wisconsin and Minnesota
Grows up to 25 ft tall
Leaves 3–4 ins long

Cherry Trees

The leaves of cherry trees tend to be longer and slightly narrower than those of apple trees. But the best way to tell them apart is by the bark. Most cherry trees have horizontal bands on the bark, while apple trees have ridged, scaly bark.

Black Cherry

You may see Black Cherry growing wild or planted in parks and gardens. It is larger than other cherry trees and differs from them in several ways. Its white flowers grow in long spikes and its dark gray bark becomes ridged and scaly with age. However, if you crush a leaf, or part of the bark, you will find it smells of cherries. The wood is used for furniture, paneling, and toys, and a cough medicine, called wild cherry syrup, is made from the bark. The small, dark, juicy cherries are made into jelly and wine.

Native to southeastern Canada and eastern US
Grows up to 80 ft tall
Leaves 2–5 ins long

Pin Cherry

This small tree is sometimes called Fire Cherry because it often shoots up on land cleared by forest fires. Look for the shiny, red twigs and long, thin leaves. The white flowers have long stalks and grow in clusters of three to five. Although the bright red cherries taste sour, they make good jelly and are eaten by birds and animals.

Native to almost all of Canada and south through Appalachians to Georgia and Colorado
Grows up to 30 ft tall
Leaves 2¹/₂–4¹/₂ ins long

Chokecherry

You can see this small tree or shrub growing along streams and roads, on mountains, and in forest clearings. Its leaves are shorter and more oval than the other wild cherries. The shiny, dark red cherries are so sour they will make you choke, which is how the tree gets its name. They can, however, be made into jelly. Look for the silvery webs of tent caterpillars among the twigs.

Native to much of Canada and US, except in parts of the South
Grows up to 20 ft tall
Leaves 1¹/₂–3¹/₄ ins long

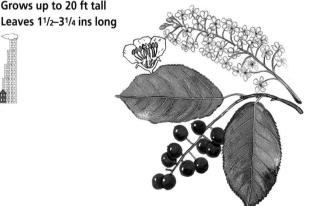

All the cherry trees on this page have been introduced. They are planted for their blossom, not for their fruit.

Pissard's Purple Plum

This is a form of plum tree, known as a cherry plum. The pink buds open up into starry, white flowers. Notice how they grow singly, not in clusters. They are followed by purple or brownish red leaves.

Introduced from Iran
Planted in city suburbs, especially in
western US and British Columbia
Grows up to 33 ft tall – Leaves 2½ ins long

Weeping Rosebud Cherry

You can recognize this tree from its drooping branches and the delicate, pink flowers, which cover it in March. Look for it in large yards and parks near either coast.

Introduced from Japan
Planted in East from Massachusetts
to Washington and in
Ohio, Washington,
and British Columbia
Grows up to 50 ft tall
Leaves 7–8 ins long

Japanese Cherry "Shirotae"

This is the first Japanese cherry to flower. It has single, white flowers and bright green leaves.

Introduced from Japan
Planted in parks and botanic
gardens in New York,
Victoria, and Seattle
Grows up to 30 ft tall
Leaves 7–8 ins long

Japanese Cherry "Kwanzan"

Japanese cherries are not often planted in North America, but this is probably the most common one. You cannot mistake its clusters of florid, pink flowers. Like all Japanese cherries, it has shiny, red bark with many horizontal stripes.

Introduced from Japan
Grows up to 40 ft tall
Leaves 4–6 ins long

Trees with Pods of Seeds

All of these trees, except the Tallowtree, produce pods of seeds, just like peas do. Look at the trees on page 29 because they produce pods too.

Voss's Golden Chaintree

This small, yard tree is a hybrid of Laburnum and Scottish Laburnum. You cannot miss it in spring when it is hung with long catkins of yellow flowers. The flowers give way to pods of poisonous, black seeds. The leaves are divided into three oval leaflets.

Most common in British Colombia, Idaho, and Washington
Grows up to 26 ft tall
Leaves 2¹/₂–3¹/₂ ins long

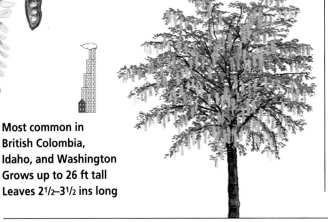

Eastern Redbud

You will see this small, bushy tree growing wild in woods as well as planted in city streets and gardens. It is at its best in early spring, before the leaves come out, when it is covered with clusters of rose-pink flowers. They can be eaten in salads or fried. They give way to thin, flat pods, which are pink at first, but turn blackish as they ripen. Look too for the dull green, heart-shaped leaves.

Native to much of eastern US
Grows up to 40 ft tall
Leaves 2¹/₂–4¹/₂ ins long

Tallowtree

Tallowtree does not produce pods of seeds, but it does have clusters of tiny, yellow-green flowers on stout, 4-inch spikes. You can tell them from a golden chaintree by their leaves and fruit. The simple leaves look rather like those of poplar, round with a long point. The flowers turn into brown seeds, which split open in fall to show white, waxy seeds. The Chinese used them to make candles.

Introduced from China
Grows wild in southern US states.
scarce in Southwest
Grows up to 30 ft tall
Leaves 1¹/₂–3 ins long

Pagoda Tree

This street tree is common in towns and parks in the South. It looks rather like a Black Locust, but its white flowers do not come out until late summer. They give way to narrow, yellowish pods, which shrink between the seeds so they look like strings of beads. The leaves consist of paired leaflets, which have a strange smell when you crush them. Notice how the branches twist in the weeping form of the tree. Pagoda Trees get their name because they are often planted around temples in eastern Asia.

Introduced from China and Korea
Planted across US in the north
Grows up to 60 ft tall
Leaves 6–10 ins long

Silk-tree

You will easily recognize this tree from its fern-like leaves and pink flowers. The flowers stay on the tree all summer and look like balls of long threads. The tree is also called Mimosa because the leaves fold up at night. (The leaves of true Mimosa fold up when touched.) Notice the shape of the tree—it has a broad, flat crown.

Introduced from Asia
Planted in southeastern
US & west to Texas
Grows up to 20 ft tall
Leaves 6–15 ins long

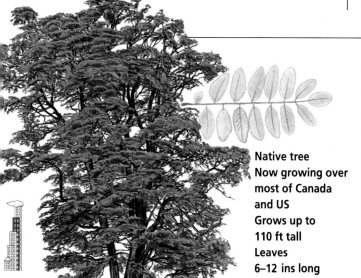

Native tree
Now growing over most of Canada and US
Grows up to 110 ft tall
Leaves 6–12 ins long

Black Locust

You are most likely to notice Black Locust trees in late spring when the hanging clusters of white, fragrant flowers are out. They give way to narrow, flat, dark brown pods of beans. Look too at the leaves. The pairs of leaflets fold up at night. But be careful as the twigs are covered with pairs of short spines. Native Americans used the wood to make bows, and the first colonists used it for the corner posts of their houses.

Magnolias & Others

Magnolias have large, spectacular flowers. Look at the leaves as well as the flowers to tell them apart. Southern Catalpa and Royal Paulownia also have attractive flowers.

Cucumbertree

Cucumbertree belongs to the magnolia family, but is named after the shape of its fruit. It has bell-shaped flowers with greenish yellow or bright yellow petals. They are about 3 inches wide and turn into dark red, cucumber-shaped fruits, about 3 inches long. The fruits split open as they ripen in late summer. Look then for seeds hanging on long threads. The oval leaves end in a short point and sometimes have wavy edges.

Native to southeastern Canada and eastern and southern US
Grows up to 80 ft tall – Leaves 5–10 ins long

Sweetbay

Look for this magnolia tree in coastal swamps and beside ponds and river. It has sweet-smelling flowers, which open into white cups in late spring and early summer. In fall look for the red, cone-like fruits among the shiny green leaves. Crush one of the leaves and sniff its spicy smell. Although Sweetbay loses its leaves in northern winters, it is almost evergreen in the South.

Native to Gulf and East Coasts
Grows up to 60 ft tall – Leaves 3–6 ins long

Southern Magnolia

Southern Magnolia has very large, white flowers. They may be up to 10 inches across and are bigger than those of any other native tree. Notice how the thick evergreen leaves turn under slightly at the edges. They are shiny, bright green above, but are covered with orange-brown hairs below.

Native in extreme South
Planted farther north and west: California to BC
Grows up to 80 ft tall – Leaves 5–8 ins long

Saucer Magnolia

Saucer Magnolia is the most common yard magnolia. Its large flowers may be pink, purple, or white. They are tulip-shaped at first, but open wider into saucers. Look for the red seeds in early fall, when the long, cone-like fruits split open. You can tell Chinese magnolias from native ones because they flower before their leaves open, whereas American magnolias flower after their leaves open.

Hybrid of Chinese and
Japanese trees
Planted widely across US
Grows up to 25 ft tall
Leaves 5–8 ins long

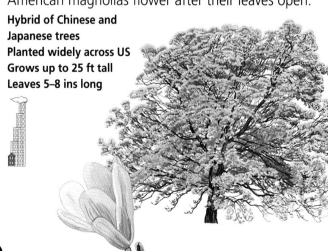

Royal Paulownia

Look for Royal Paulownia on waste ground and roadsides as well as in city squares, parks and gardens. Be careful not to confuse it with Catalpa. It has enormous leaves and pale violet, bell-shaped flowers. The hairy, brown flower buds form in late summer. Look for them on the tree in winter. The flowers are followed by egg-shaped seed capsules. As they ripen the capsules turn from green to brown, and split open to release the winged seeds.

Introduced from China
Now grows wild in eastern and southern US
Grows up to 50 ft tall
Leaves 6–16 ins long

Southern Catalpa

Southern Catalpa has large, heart-shaped leaves, which smell unpleasant when you crush them. Look for the clusters of white flowers in mid-summer. Each bell-shaped flower has two orange stripes and many purple spots and stripes. They turn into long, narrow, cigar-shaped pods, which stay on the tree all winter. When they split in two around October, look for the brown seeds with papery wings.

Native to southern US
Planted in parks
and gardens in
Canada and US
Grows up to 50 ft tall
Leaves 5–10 ins long

Umbrella Magnolia

You can recognize this tree by its very long leaves and large, white flowers. The spreading leaves are said to look like the ribs of an umbrella. The flowers have an unpleasant smell. Notice how the three green sepals are longer than the petals.

Native to
mountain valleys
and forests in
eastern US
Grows up to
40 ft tall
Leaves
10–20 ins long

Other Ornamental Trees

The trees on this page are planted for their attractive flowers, fruits, or fall colors.

Black Tupelo

You can recognize Black Tupelo from its shiny, oval, green leaves, which turn bright red in fall, and from its shape. It is tall with many slender, horizontal branches. The greenish flowers develop into blue-black fruits, which look like berries. They are sour but juicy, and many birds and animals love them.

Native to southeastern Canada and eastern and southern US
Grows up to 100 ft tall
Leaves 2–5 ins long

Golden Raintree

Golden Raintree has big leaves, made up of many toothed leaflets. The yellow flowers turn into bright pink or red fruits, which are hollow except for three black seeds. The Formosan Golden Raintree is more common in the South. Look out for flowers and dull purple fruits on the tree at the same time.

Introduced from eastern Asia
Planted in parks and squares in eastern US and on West Coast
Grows up to 50 ft tall
Leaves 8–16 ins long

Crapemyrtle

You will only see Crapemyrtle's bright pink or white flowers in places with long, hot summers. They are followed by small, red berries. Look too at the bark. It is pink and gray, with flecks of green and pink, and is very smooth.

Introduced from China and Korea
Planted around the Coastal Plain and along Mississippi Valley
Grows up to 30 ft tall
Leaves 2½ ins long

Flowering Dogwood

This tree is spectacular in spring and fall. Look carefully at the flowers in spring. At the center of the white "petals" is a cluster of tiny, yellow-green flowers each with its own true petals. By fall the tiny flowers have developed into clusters of shiny, red berries and the leaves have turned red below. The rough bark is reddish brown. Native Americans used it in a cure for malaria.

Native to southeastern Canada and eastern US
Grows up to 30 ft tall
Leaves 2½–5 ins long

The trees on this page are similar to the elms and ashes shown on pages 12 and 25. These trees, however, are often planted in yards for shade or ornament.

Siberian Elm

Siberian Elms grow well in dry places. In parts of Arizona and New Mexico they are the only tree you will see. They are planted to give shade at every rest-station. Look for them too in cities as far north as Winnipeg and throughout the US east of the Rocky Mountains. Be careful not to confuse it with Chinese Elm. It flowers in early spring and produces rounder seeds than Chinese Elm, but the best way to tell them apart is by the bark. Siberian Elm has rough, gray or brown bark.

Introduced from Asia
Grows wild on Great Plains,
but planted elsewhere too
Grows up to 60 ft tall
Leaves 3/4–2 ins long

American Mountain Ash

This small tree has clusters of white flowers in spring followed by red berries in fall. Watch for cedar waxwings and grouse feeding on the berries. Moose prefer to eat the leaves and winter twigs. Look for the glossy, sticky buds in winter. They are red on top and green underneath. They open up into leaves with many pairs of toothed leaflets.

Native to northeastern North America from
Newfoundland to Appalachians
Grows up to 30 ft tall – Leaves 6–8 ins long

Chinese Elm

The most unusual thing about this tree is that it produces its small, greenish flowers in fall. Look for them at the base of the leaves. They quickly change into oval seeds held in a pale yellow, oval wing. The dark green leaves are oval too. They are shiny on top with teeth like a saw around the edge. Perhaps the most attractive part of the tree is its bark. It is pale blue-grey, mottled with brown, and flakes off to show the inner red bark underneath.

Introduced from China, Korea, and Japan
Planted across US, particularly around Gulf of Mexico and on West Coast
Grows up to 50 ft tall
leaves 3/4–2 ins long

From Flower To Seed

Some trees have male flowers and others female flowers. The male flowers produce millions of grains of pollen, which are blown in the wind or carried by insects to the female flowers on another tree. Some trees have male and female parts within the same flower. When the right kind of pollen lands on the sticky stigma of the female flower it grows a tube down to the ovary where it joins with a female egg to produce a new seed.

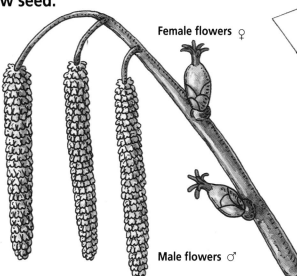

Female flowers ♀

Male flowers ♂

Scattering seeds

Most ripe seeds fall onto the ground underneath the tree, but they have a better chance of growing if they are scattered away from the parent tree.

Many berries are eaten by birds and squirrels who drop the seeds far from the tree. Squirrels and mice bury stores of nuts in the ground to get them through the winter, but some nuts survive to grow into new trees. The wind blows winged seeds onto new ground.

Make a winged seed

1 **Copy this shape** onto a piece of paper.
2 **Cut down the center line and fold** one wing one way and the other the opposite way.
3 **Pin a paper clip onto the other end.**

Looking for flowers

All trees have flowers. They need them to make seeds. Some flowers are small and hard to spot, and some are not colored or shaped as you might expect. Look out for the different kinds of flowers.

4 **Stand on a chair** and let the shape go. What happens? Does it always twist the same way?

5 **Experiment** with longer and shorter wings, with two or more paper clips, with wider and narrower stems. Which design flies best?

Collecting fruits

Trees hide their seeds inside fruits. There are many different kinds to collect—for example, berries from mountain ash, cherry, and hawthorn; nuts from chestnut, beech, oak, hickory, walnut, and others; winged seeds from sycamore, maple, gray birch, and elm. London planes produce round, spiky fruits while golden chaintrees, black locust, and eastern redbuds produce pods of seeds. All the conifers produce woody cones of seeds.

Mountain ash berries

Beech nut

Winged sycamore seed

Horse chestnut conker

Black cherry has bright, sweet-smelling flowers to attract insects.

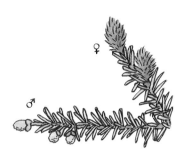

Silver fir has upright female cone flowers and smaller male cone flowers under the branches.

London plane has round female flowers and clusters of yellow male flowers on the same tree.

Redbud pod

Woody pine cone

Evergreens & Conifers

The trees on the first six pages of this section are evergreen broad-leaved trees. Unlike the trees in the earlier sections, they do not lose their leaves in winter. All of the conifers, except for those on page 65, are evergreen too. You can recognize a conifer very quickly by its leaves. Generally, they are thin and sharp, like needles, or cling to the branch like scales.

Most of the trees in the West and in northern Canada are conifers. Do not be surprised to see them in the South too, along with palms and eucalyptus trees. Evergreens can survive very cold and very hot weather better than deciduous trees. Broad-leaved evergreens often have leathery, shiny leaves which stop them drying out.

Conifer needles have very little surface area, so they do not lose much water. Conifers belong to an ancient, primitive group of plants that evolved before the flowering plants. A few form their seeds very slowly, taking many years. While they develop some are protected inside a cone. The shape and size of the cone can help to identify the tree.

The conifer trees (pages 58–77) have been arranged according to their fruits and leaves. Those at the beginning do not have cones. They are followed by trees with scaly leaves, and then by trees with single needles. The last trees to be shown are the pines, which have bundles of long, thin needles. The picture shows seven trees from this book. How many can you recognize?

Leyland Cypress, Pacific Silver Fir, Variegated Holly, Western Hemlock, Monkey Puzzle, Spruce Pine, English Yew.

Holly & Others

You can easily recognize some hollies from their shiny, prickly leaves.

European Holly

European Holly usually has buckled leaves, unlike the flat ones of American Holly. European Holly has smaller, shinier leaves and the berries are shinier too. There are many varieties of European Holly. Their leaves are different colors or shapes and some have larger berries. As its name suggests, the Yellow-berried Holly has yellow berries.

Introduced from southern Europe, north Africa, and west Asia
Planted across the US, mainly in states near the coasts
Grows up to 50 ft tall
Leaves 1¼–2¾ ins long

Possumhaw

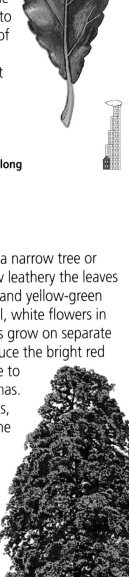

You are most likely to notice Possumhaw in winter when its gray twigs are covered with small, red berries. Watch for opossums, raccoons, songbirds, and other animals feeding on the berries. You might be surprised to hear that this tree is a member of the holly family. Its leaves are toothed rather than spiny, and it drops most of them in fall, although a few may remain on some young shoots.

Native to southeastern US
Grows up to 20 ft tall – Leaves 1–3 ins long

American Holly

You may see American Holly as a narrow tree or clipped into hedges. Notice how leathery the leaves are. They are dark green above and yellow-green below. Look for clusters of small, white flowers in spring. Male and female flowers grow on separate trees, so only female trees produce the bright red berries, which people like to use to decorate their homes at Christmas. Watch for songbirds, game birds, and other animals feeding on the bitter-tasting berries.

Native to southeastern US
and north to Massachusetts
Grows up to 70 ft tall
Leaves 2–4 ins long

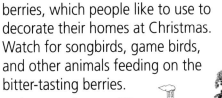

Box

Box can grow as a tree, but it is more common as a bush or a hedge. It is a good tree for topiary, so you may see it clipped into various shapes. Look for the small, yellow flowers in spring. They are followed by brown, woody capsules, each with three seeds.

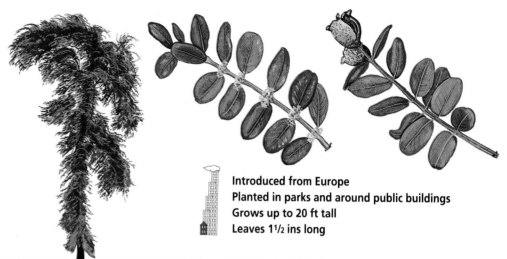

Introduced from Europe
Planted in parks and around public buildings
Grows up to 20 ft tall
Leaves 1½ ins long

Tanoak

Tanoaks are similar to Golden Chinkapins, but their leaves have toothed edges and they produce acorns, not spiky seed capsules. Do not confuse it with the oak trees shown on pages 16 and 17.

Native to the West Coast
Grows up to 150 ft tall
Leaves 3 ins long

Golden Chinkapin

Golden Chinkapin is similar to American Chestnut (see page 21). The long, yellow clusters of flowers are male. Look for them in midsummer. The female catkins turn into spiny seed capsules. The leaves are long and oval, but do not have a toothed edge like the American Chestnut.
They are shiny, dark green above and golden below.

Native to West Coast of US
Grows up to 100 ft tall
Leaves 3 ins long

Eucalyptus & Others

Eucalyptus and Russian Olives mostly have long, thin leaves.

Bluegum Eucalyptus

You can recognize eucalyptus trees from the spicy smell they give when you crush one of their long leaves. You can tell Bluegums from their big blue-white seed capsules and light brown bark, which peels off in long strips, leaving smooth, blue-gray bark below. It has flowers and fruits on it all year round. The young leaves are nearly round and grow in pairs, although the adult leaves always grow alternately. The flowers are covered by a hard capsule that opens to let the yellow stamens stick out. Look under the tree for the blue-white seed capsules.

Introduced from Tasmania
Now grows wild along West Coast of US
Grows up to 200 ft tall
Leaves 8–10 ins long

Red Gum Eucalyptus

Red Gum is also called Longbeak Eucalyptus. It is less dark and heavy than Bluegum, and its bark is white or gray with deep ridges. Look for the clusters of white flowers. They give way to small, brown seed capsules, that look like five-pointed stars.

Introduced from Australia
Grows in California east to Arizona
Grows up to 120 ft tall
Leaves 5–6 ins long

Silver Dollar Tree

This is the only eucalyptus tree you will see in the East of the US outside southern Florida. You can easily recognize it from its round, bright, blue-white leaves.

Introduced from Australia
Grown in southern and southwestern US
Up to 80 ft tall – Leaves 4–5 ins long

Pacific Madrone

You may see this tree growing in woods on low mountains, and in towns, parks, and gardens. New shoots are yellow-green, but turn to bright orange and then to deep red as the bark becomes thicker. The underside of the leaves are blue-white. The white clusters of flowers are followed by green berries, which change to orange and then scarlet.

Native to Pacific Coast from Vancouver Island to Los Angeles
Grows up to 100 ft tall
Leaves 2–6 ins long

Russian Olive

Russian Olive is easy to recognize because its leaves, twigs, and fruit are covered with silvery scales. Even its yellow, bell-shaped flowers are silvery on the outside. In spite of its name, Russian Olive is not related to the olive tree, although it does produce sweet berries with a single stone. Watch for waxwings, robins, pheasants, and other birds feeding on them.

Introduced from southern Europe and Asia
Planted across southern Canada and US from New England to California
Grows up to 20 ft tall, but is often a shrub
Leaves 1½–3¼ ins long

California Laurel

Like gum trees, California Laurel has spicy-smelling leaves when you crush them. Do not sniff them for too long though, or they will give you a headache. They can, however, be used to flavor stews like bay leaves.

Native to West Coast states: Oregon and California
Grows up to 120 ft tall
Leaves up to 6 ins long

Palms & Palm-like Trees

Palms are easy to recognize. They have a single trunk with no branches and large, spreading leaves. They differ from other trees because they have no heartwood and show no annual rings in their trunks.

Cabbage Palmetto

Cabbage Palmettos have fan-shaped leaves, which spread out around the top of the trunk. The leaves are dark green and shiny, and are deeply cut into many slender strips. The fragrant, white flowers are followed by clusters of shiny, black berries. The leaves are made into baskets and hats, and the leafstalks into brooms. The trunks are used for wharf pilings, docks, and posts.

Native to Florida and southeastern coast of US
Widely planted in streets and parks in southern and southwestern towns
Grows up to 50 ft tall
Leaves 4–7 ft long

Chusan Palm

This palm can grow in much colder climates than other palms, but is uncommon in North America. Its fan-like leaves often turn bright yellow before they are shed. Notice how hairy and scaly its bark is.

Introduced from China
Planted in parts of California and Oregon
Grows up to 30 ft tall
Leaves 4 ft wide

California Washingtonia

This tree is also called California Fan Palm. It is easy to recognize from the way its green leaves rise out of the frill of dead leaves around the top of the trunk. The bark is reddish brown and smoother than other palms. Look for the scars where dead leafstalks have fallen off. The clusters of yellow flowers are 10 feet long and they remain on the tree even after they have died. The fruits are long clusters of black berries.

Native to Gulf Coast
Planted also in California
Grows up to 60 ft tall
Leaves 6 ft long on 5 ft stalks

Queen Palm

This tree is easy to recognize from the dark gray rings on its pale gray trunk. It has only about ten arching leaves at a time, rising from a green sheath.

Introduced from South America
Planted in some cities in California,
Gulf of Mexico,and Florida
Grows up to 60 ft tall – Leaves 15 ft long

Joshua Tree

It is easy to recognize a Joshua Tree from its many short, upturned branches. It was named by the Mormons who thought it looked like a man lifting his arms to heaven. Joshua Tree is a yucca, not a palm. Its dagger-like leaves end in a sharp point and are clustered at the ends of the branches. The waxy flowers give way to clusters of brown seeds. A new branch grows where each flower grew.

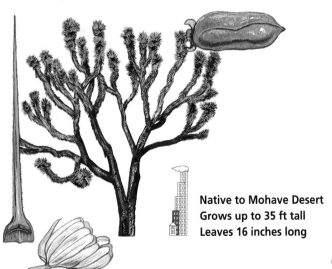

Native to Mohave Desert
Grows up to 35 ft tall
Leaves 16 inches long

Date Palm

Date Palms have dusty, dark green leaves in the shape of long plumes with many stiff leaflets. Look for the bunches of sweet, dark brown dates for which the tree is cultivated in Florida and California. You will also see many of them in the streets of Phoenix, Arizona, and the city itself is called after the tree's Latin name, *Phoenix (dactylifera)*.

Introduced from North Africa and western Asia
Planted in hot, dry parts of Florida, California and Arizona
Grows up to 100 ft tall – Leaves up to 20 ft long

Canary Palm

The Canary Palm has bright green, plume-like leaves and a tall, elegant trunk, which makes the Date Palm look dusty and dumpy by comparison. Canary Palm is sometimes called Pineapple Palm because its trunk is covered with the rough scales of dropped leaf stalks, and so looks rather like the outside of a pineapple. The flowers produce date-like fruits, but they are too dry to eat.

Introduced from the Canary Islands
Most common around Gulf of
Mexico and Californian coasts
Grows up to 60 ft tall
Leaves 15–20 ft long

More Trees Needed

Young trees are called saplings. You will see lots of them when you walk through parks and woods, or you can grow your own from pips and seeds.

Choosing a tree for planting

Do you have room in your yard for a new tree? Before you rush out to plant a bought one or one of your pot-plant saplings, think about what kind of tree would suit your yard best.

Sycamore, ash, and tree of heaven grow very large very quickly. You could soon have a monster tree in your yard, blocking out the light and pushing its roots under the walls of the house, which could damage it badly. You will find that mountain ash, gray birch, and black cherry are all attractive trees that do not grow too large.

Many trees are not grown from seed. They are grafted onto the stems of other trees and can only be bought from a tree nursery. They are more expensive than growing your own saplings, but they have been specially produced for yards.

Grow your own

1 **In autumn collect seeds** from trees like oak, ash, gray birch, and cypress.
2 **Soak the seeds overnight** then peel off their tough outer skin.

3 **Plant several seeds from one tree in a pot of compost.** Cover with more compost and water well.
4 **Leave the pots in a cool place** and wait to see what happens. Don't let the compost dry out.

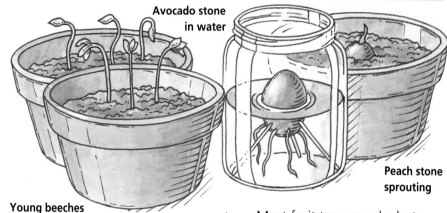

Avocado stone in water

Young beeches

Peach stone sprouting

Exotic trees

The next time you eat some fruit—apple, pear, orange, cherry, or peach—save the pips and pits. Soak them in water for a few days, then plant a few of each kind in a small pot of compost. Water the pot well and leave in a cool place.

Avocados have large stones. Soak one in water for a week as shown above, then plant it in a pot of compost with its tip just showing above the surface.

Most fruit trees need a hot, sunny climate. If any of yours grow, put them in a hot, sunny place, or in a greenhouse. Much of the fruit we eat has few or no pips at all. The trees they came from were grown from grafts and are not very fertile. So, don't be disappointed if many of these seeds do not grow.

Planting your tree

1 **Use a yard of string and two pins** to mark a circle on the ground.

2 **Dig a hole about 2 feet deep.** Loosen any stones or hard earth at the bottom of the hole.

3 **Line the bottom of the hole** with leaf mold or manure to about 6 inches deep.

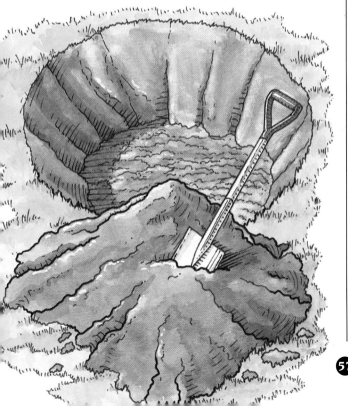

4 **Push a short stake or post into the hole.** This will support the tree against wind and accidents.

5 **Take the tree out of its container and hold it in place in the center of the hole.** Spread out the roots and fill in around them with a mixture of soil, compost, and sand.

6 **Tread the top soil down firmly and rake it over gently.** Tie the tree to the stake with at least two proper plastic tree ties. Water the tree well and wait for it to grow.

7 **Check from time to time** that the ties are not cutting into the tree. You can remove the stake after about two years.

Ask an adult to help with the digging.

Ginkgo, Yews, & Others

The trees on these two pages are all conifers, but are unusual in different ways. Most of them, for example, produce berry-like fruits instead of woody cones.

Ginkgo

The Ginkgo is sometimes called a living fossil. It flourished 200 million years ago when dinosaurs roamed the earth, but died out everywhere except in China. It was introduced into America in the eighteenth century, and is often planted in city streets where it stands up well to air pollution, pests, and disease. Gingkos are easy to recognize from their fan-shaped leaves and small, soft fruits. The fruits smell awful when they rot, so male trees are usually planted. They are sometimes called Maidenhair Trees because their leaves look like maidenhair ferns.

Introduced from China
Planted from Montreal
to New Orleans and
west to Pacific Coast
Grows up to
100 ft tall
Leaves
1–2 ins long

Pacific Yew

This yew tree likes the shade of damp woods. It has flat, pointed needles and red berries like the English Yew. The best way to tell them apart is by whether it is growing in the West or East. Notice too the shape of the tree. In inland woods, Pacific Yew grows only as a shrub.

Native to West
Coast from Alaska
to California
Grows up to 50 ft tall
Leaves up to
1½ ins long

English Yew

Yews are very primitive, but hardy trees that can live for thousands of years. Look for the red, berry-like fruits, and the single, flat, pointed needles, but be careful. The seeds and leaves are poisonous to people and to most animals except deer and rabbits.

Introduced from Europe
Planted in eastern Canada
and US south to
District of Columbia
Grows up to 65 ft tall
Leaves up to
1½ ins long

Monkey Puzzle

You can easily recognize a Monkey Puzzle by the way the leaves grow in an interlocking spiral around the branches. The tree gets its name from the difficulty any monkey would have in climbing up through the sharp leaves. Male and female flowers usually grow on separate trees. Look for the thick, drooping, male catkins on trees, which do not produce the large, spiny cones.

Introduced from Chile
Planted in western states
from British Columbia
to California
Grows up to 80 ft tall
Leaves 2 ins long

California Torreya

California Torreya belongs to the yew family and, like yew trees, has single, flat needles. It is sometimes called California Nutmeg because its fleshy fruits look like true nutmegs. They have purple stripes when they are ripe. Split one open to see the hard seed inside.

Native to parts of California
Grows up to 50 ft tall
Leaves 3 ins long

Bigleaf Podocarp

The leaves of many Podocarps look like those of yew, but their fruits are different. Some produce cones with fleshy scales, while the Bigleaf Podocarp produces green, plum-like fruits. They are also known as Yellowwoods.

Introduced from New Zealand or from China or Japan
Planted from South Carolina to southern California
Grows up to 50 ft tall
Leaves 2–4 ins long

Junipers & Redcedars

All the trees on these two pages belong to the cypress family. Apart from Common Juniper, all cypresses have scale-like leaves. Like yews, junipers produce berry-like fruits instead of cones. You can tell them from yews (see page 58) by their scale-like leaves and the shape of the tree.

Common Juniper

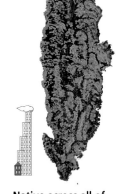

Juniper is the most widespread conifer in North America. Although it sometimes grows into a small tree in New England, you will see it only as a shrub elsewhere. The whitish-blue, berry-like cones take two to three years to ripen, so you will always see some on the bush. Watch for grouse, pheasants, and bobwhites feeding on them. They are also used to make gin. Look too for the tiny, yellow, male flowers and notice how the needles grow in clusters of three along the stems.

Native across all of Canada and parts of US
Grows up to 25 ft tall, but is usually a shrub of 1–4 ft
Leaves up to 1/2 ins long

Utah Juniper

This tree is very common around the Grand Canyon and the deserts from Wyoming to California. You cannot mistake its candelabra-like shape. Look too for its gray-brown, striped bark.

Native to deserts of southwestern US
Grows up to 20 ft tall
Leaves 1/2–1 ins long

Meyer's Blue Juniper

This juniper grows very quickly. Look for the pink-brown bark which peels off in papery flakes, and for the blue-green needles.

Introduced from China
Planted in yards in British Columbia, Washington and Ohio
Grows up to 25 ft tall
Leaves 1/2–1 ins long

Eastern Redcedar

Eastern Redcedar is the most common juniper tree east of the Rocky Mountains. It can stand up to extreme heat and cold. You can tell it from other junipers by its tall, thin shape. It has scale-like leaves: some are prickly, and some flat and smooth. The soft, berry-like cones are sweet and juicy. Watch for waxwings and other birds that like to feed on them. The trees are planted for shelter and for Christmas trees. The wood is used to make cedar chests, fence posts, and carvings. Oil from the leaves and wood is used in medicines and perfumes. The Rocky Mountain Juniper looks very like it, but grows only to the west of the Prairie States.

Native to eastern US
Grows up to 60 ft tall
Leaves 1/2 ins long

The trees on this page have an aromatic and resinous smell.

Western Redcedar

Apart from its huge size, you can recognize this cypress from its cones. Each has ten to twelve scales and is flask-shaped. In damp weather you will easily smell the heavy, fruity scent of its scale-like leaves. Like the Northern White Cedar, the wood was used by Native Americans to make canoes. It is light and strong and does not rot in water. They also used it for totem poles, houses, boxes, and buckets. Today it is made into shingles (wooden roof tiles).

Native to western states from Alaska to California
Can be over 200 ft tall
Scale-like leaves about ¹/₂ ins long

Northern White Cedar

Northern White Cedar grows very slowly and can live for 400 years or more. Turn the yellow-green leaves over to see their pale, matt yellow-green underside. If you crush them, they will smell of apple. Look for the smooth, brown cones at the ends of the stronger shoots. Native Americans used the strong, light wood to build canoes. Today the wood is used mainly for posts and poles. The twigs are used to make cedar oil for medicines.

Native to eastern Canada,
northeastern US,
and west to Illinois
Grows up to 70 ft tall
Scale-like leaves about ¹/₈ ins long

Oriental Arborvitae

The best way to tell this tree from other cypresses is by its shape. It often has branches sprouting from the bottom of the trunk. In China, the scented branches are used in New Year celebrations. But if you crush the leaves, they give only a faint scent. You cannot miss its many cones—they are blue-white in summer, but turn dark brown. Look for the large, hooked beaks on about four of the scales. There are many different varieties, including one with golden leaves. Arborvitae means "tree of life."

Introduced from China
Planted across US,
especially in southeastern states
Grows up to 25 ft tall
Scale-like leaves about
¹/₈ ins long

Cypresses

Some cypresses are called cedars, but you can tell they are cypresses by their scaly leaves. There are two kinds of cypress trees. "True" cypresses have big cones, and "false" cypresses have small cones and leaves in flattened sprays.

Smooth Cypress

The best way to recognize this tree is by its bark. It is smooth and dark purple at first. Then it flakes off to leave pale yellow and dark red patches below. The leaves are sometimes speckled with spots of white resin. Crush them to get the smell of pineapples.

Native to Arizona
Planted in Central Valley and other places in US
Grows up to 70 ft tall
Scale-like leaves about 1/8 ins long

Incense Cedar

This cypress is named after its sweet-smelling wood and foliage, burned as incense. It is most closely related to the Western Redcedar (see page 61) and is similar in shape to it. Look for the long, narrow, red-brown cones to tell them apart.

Native to Oregon and California
Planted elsewhere in US
Grows up to 180 ft or more tall
Leaves 1/2 ins long

Italian Cypress

The leaves and cones of Italian Cypress look much like those of Monterey Cypress, but you can easily tell them apart by their shape. Italian Cypresses grow in narrow columns, often with a pointed top.

Introduced from Greece
Planted in southern states southern California, and Arizona
Grows up to 60 ft tall
Scale-like leaves about 1/8 ins long

Monterey Cypress

You can tell Monterey Cypress from the lemon scent of its crushed leaves. Some wild trees grow in strange shapes. Long, slender branches covered thickly with leaves look like ropes. Look for the cones. They are almost 2 inches across and roughly round with eight to ten scales. Notice how the scales are shaped like shields. Both Monterey Cypress and Italian Cypress are liable to be attacked and killed by a fungal disease. They are sometimes replaced by the hardier Leyland Cypress.

Native to California in three tiny groups
Planted near sea to North
Grows up to 115 ft tall
Scale-like leaves about 1/8 ins long

The trees on this page are all false cypresses.

Port Orford Cedar

This tree now comes in many shapes and sizes. There are about 250 varieties, with leaves that vary in color from blue to gray, green, and gold. The leaves of wild trees are dark yellow-green. Crush them to smell their parsley-scented resin. Look for the dark red, male cones and bluish-green, female cones growing on the same tree. In Europe it is called Lawson Cypress.

Native to California–Oregon border
Planted along West Coast
Grows up to 200 ft tall
Leaves ³/₄ ins long

Atlantic White Cedar

This tree gets its name from its pale green leaves with white marks near their base. When you crush them, they smell of ginger. The wood is so long-lasting that fallen trees which have been buried for many years can still be used to make shingles (wooden roof tiles).

Native to swamps on East Coast
Grows up to 50 ft tall
Leaves less than ¹/₈ ins long

Alaska Cedar

The best way to tell this tree from other cypresses is by the hooked spikes on its small, round cones. The tree itself is cone-shaped with dark, hanging branchlets. When you crush the leaves they smell of turpentine. In winter and spring look for the pale yellow, male flowers.

Native to Alaska and western states
Grows up to 100 ft tall
Leaves ¹/₈ ins long

Leyland Cypress

There are several different varieties of Leyland Cypress. Some have lighter leaves than others. They have all been developed for growing in gardens. They grow tall very quickly and are often planted to make a thick hedge or screen. Notice how the leaves cover the tree right down to the ground.

Hybrid of Alaska Cedar and Monterey Cypress
Grows up to 130 ft tall
Scale-like leaves about ¹/₂ ins long

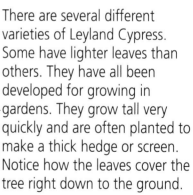

Redwoods & Larches

Although they carry the names of various other trees—cedar, cypress, and fir—all the trees on this page are redwoods. Redwoods are large, beautiful trees. They have thick, fibrous, red barks and small, woody cones with scales shaped like shields.

Giant Sequoia

Giant Sequoias are not quite the tallest trees in the world, but they are the most massive and also the oldest. "General Sherman" is 270 feet tall and measures 82 feet around the trunk. "Grizzly Giant" is thought to be over 3,500 years old. Giant Sequoias have deep roots and thick bark, which allows them to survive gales and forest fires. In fact, they need forest fires to thrive. The heat opens their cones and releases their seeds, and also makes space for new Sequoias to grow. Notice the leaves which do not cling to the branches as closely as those of cypresses.

Native to California
Planted north to Vancouver
Grows up to 290 ft tall
Leaves 1/2 ins long

Chinese Fir

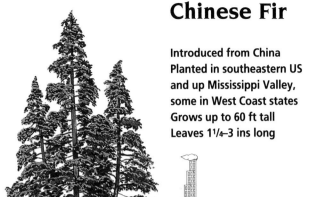

Introduced from China
Planted in southeastern US and up Mississippi Valley, some in West Coast states
Grows up to 60 ft tall
Leaves 1 1/4–3 ins long

Coast Redwood

The tallest Coast Redwood measured is 372 feet, and is the tallest tree in the world. The trees grow tall in the moist sea-fogs that cling to the hills just back from the coast of California. The thick bark is very soft and fibrous. It is bright red on young trees but darker and ridged on older trees.

Native to California
Grows over 350 ft tall
Leaves 1/2–3/4 ins long

Chinese Fir is similar to Coast Redwood. You can tell them apart by their leaves. Chinese Fir needles are much longer and broader than those of Coast Redwood and they narrow to a sharp point. Look for the spiny cones and for the rusty, dead leaves among the bright green, new leaves in the crown of the tree.

Japanese Redcedar

This redwood thrives best in cool, wet summers, although it never grows as tall here as it does in China and Japan. Look for its spaced, horizontal branches, which sometimes form billowing clumps.

**Introduced from China and Japan
Planted on East Coast and places on West Coast
Grows up to 100 ft tall
Leaves about ¹/₂ ins long**

The trees below belong to the larch family and are deciduous—that is, they lose their leaves in winter.

Western Larch

Western Larch is the biggest larch of all. Its bright green needles grow in rosettes of thirty to forty leaves on old twigs and singly on new twigs. They turn golden-yellow before they drop in fall. Look too for the whiskery cones.

**Native to Rocky Mountains from British Columbia to Montana
Grows up to 220 ft tall
Leaves up to 2 ins long**

Tamarack

This is the most northerly conifer in North America. It grows right across Canada and as far north as trees can grow. The needles are bright green and grow in rosettes of twelve to twenty, except on new shoots where they grow singly. Look for the flaking, pink-brown bark. Native Americans used the slender roots to sew birch bark for their canoes.

**Native to Alaska, Canada, and northeastern US
Grows up to 80 ft tall
Leaves 1 ins long**

Bald Cypress

Look for Bald Cypress in wet soil, along riverbanks, and beside lakes. When its roots are submerged in water, it grows "knees"—broad pillars 20 yards or more from the tree, which reach about 5 feet high and through which the roots can breathe oxygen. It is sometimes called the "wood eternal" because it does not rot. The wood has been used to build bridges, docks, boats, and warehouses.

**Native to southeastern US, and up the Mississippi to Illinois
Grows up to 120 ft tall
Leaves ¹/₂–³/₄ ins long**

Firs & True Cedars

Fir trees have single, blunt needles and, except for the Douglas Fir, their cones stand upright. Cedars also have upright cones.

White Fir

Look closely at the needles of White Fir. They are blue-green with blue-gray stripes on both sides of the leaf. When you crush them, they smell of lemons. Notice how they curve upward from the twigs. Look too for the yellow or red flowers which open in spring.

Native to eastern Rocky Mountains from Idaho to Mexico
Grows up to 130 ft tall
Leaves 2 ins long

Grand Fir

Grand Firs grow very quickly and were once the tallest silver firs. To tell this fir from others, look for its flat sprays of needles which smell of oranges when crushed. You will find it hard to see the cones. They grow only near the crown on trees which are more than about a hundred feet tall. The cones break up on the tree, so you will not find them on the ground.

Native to West Coast from British Columbia to California
Grows up to 200 ft tall
Leaves 2 ins long

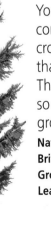

Pacific Silver Fir

Another name for this fir is Beautiful Fir, and it certainly lives up to its name. Like the Balsam Fir it is full of resin and the bark of young trees has resin blisters. The purple buds quickly become covered with white resin. Crush the leaves to smell the tangy, fruity scent of tangerines.

Native to West Coast from British Columbia to Oregon
Grows up to 220 ft or more tall
Leaves 1½ ins long

Balsam Fir

This fir grows into a narrow, pointed crown and is often used as a Christmas tree. The cones are purple at first, but turn brown as they ripen. Look closely at the needles. They are dark green above and have two, narrow, white bands below. Rub them to smell the aromatic scent of balsam. The tree forms large blisters of resin in the bark. This resin, called Canada Balsam, is used for mounting microscopic specimens.

Native from Alberta to Labrador and south to northern New England
Grows up to 60 ft tall
Leaves ½–1 ins long

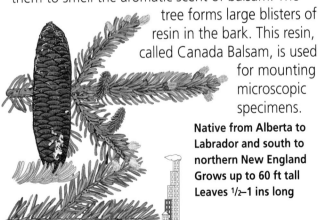

Cedars are large, magnificent trees, with needles that grow singly or in rosettes.

Douglas Fir

The Douglas Fir is not a true fir. It has hanging cones and is similar to the Hemlocks (see page 69). The tree is slender when young, but grows more rugged with clumps of hanging branches. Douglas Firs growing inland in the Rockies have bluer leaves than those near the coast. The wood is among the strongest and best in the world. It is often used in construction work.

Native to western states
Grows up to 300 ft tall
Leaves 1 ins long

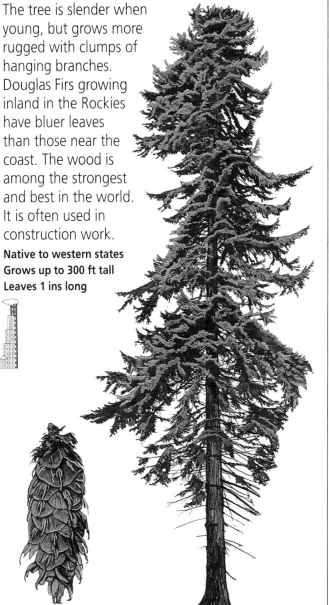

Atlas Cedar

Look for this tree in parks and gardens. In Los Angeles and San Diego it is also planted along boulevards. You are most likely to see the variety which has gray-blue needles. Notice how they form large, flat clumps. The cones are over 3 inches long and grow upright. In fall, look too for the upright, male flowers. It is also called the Blue Cedar from its color.

Introduced from North Africa
Planted in East and West
Coast states
Grows up to 130 ft tall
Leaves 1 ins long

Deodar Cedar

You can tell Deodar Cedar from Atlas Cedar because its branches spread downward to the ground Notice how the new, young shoots also hang down. Its dark green leaves are longer than those of Atlas Cedar.

Introduced from Himalayas
Planted along the
coast from Virginia
to Mississippi Valley
and along West Coast
Grows up to 130 ft tall
Leaves 2 ins long

Spruces & Hemlocks

Spruces have single, sharp needles and hanging cones. The trees themselves are cone-shaped too. Hemlocks are similar, but they have smaller cones and blunt-tipped, flattened needles.

White Spruce

This is the most important commercial tree grown in Canada. It is made into pulpwood and then into paper. It is also used for musical instruments, such as violins and pianos. The needles are shorter than those of Norway Spruce. When you crush them, they smell of skunk. Look for the shiny, light brown cones at the end of the twigs. They have smooth, thin scales and drop to the ground as they ripen.

Native to Canada, Alaska, and northern US
Grows up to 100 ft tall – Needles ½–¾ ins long

Norway Spruce

This is the most widespread exotic spruce in North America. It is planted for shade and, on both sides of the US-Canadian border, to give shelter for crops and homes from the wind sweeping across the prairies. Look for the long, hanging cones. They are up to 6 inches long, and are longer than those of any other spruce.

Introduced from Europe
Planted widely in southeastern Canada, northeastern US, Rocky Mountains, and West Coast
Grows up to 80 ft tall
Needles ½–1 ins long

Engelmann Spruce

This spruce is similar to White Spruce. You will see it from western Canada through the mountains to New Mexico and Arizona. It is often planted along roadsides, and in yards and parks. It has longer, softer needles than White Spruce, and they smell of camphor or menthol when you crush them. The ripe cones are orangey-brown with toothed edges to the scales.

Native to eastern Rocky Mountains
Grows up to 150 ft tall
Needles ¾–1 ins long

Red Spruce

Red Spruce is related to Black Spruce and sometimes forms a hybrid with it. Red Spruce has reddish brown cones and bark while Black Spruce has dull gray cones and bark. Look too at Red Spruce's bright, grassy-green needles. They are short and wiry and grow upright from the twigs. They smell of apples or candlewax when they are crushed.

Native to eastern Canada and US south to North Carolina
Grows up to 80 ft tall – Needles ¹/₂ ins long

Western & Eastern Hemlock

The Eastern Hemlock is smaller than the Western, growing only to about 70 feet tall. Colonists used to make tea from the leafy twigs of Eastern Hemlock, found from the Great Lakes to the Appalachians. With both trees look for the paler bands of color on the underside of the leaves. The new shoots of Western Hemlock droop, but straighten up as they mature. The needles grow all ways and are longer than Eastern Hemlock.

Native to West or East of North America
Western: up to 200 ft tall – Needles about ¹/₂ ins long

Black Spruce

This tree is called Black Spruce because it looks dark from a distance. You cannot mistake an old tree with its tall, thin shape and open-spaced branches. In winter, snow presses the lowest branches down to the ground. There they take root and begin to grow, so you may see a ring of saplings growing around the old tree. The dull gray cones are egg-shaped and even young trees have lots of them. Notice how the small, thin needles grow all around the pink-brown shoots. They smell of menthol cough-sweets when you crush them.

Native to Alaska, Canada, and northeastern US
Grows up to 60 ft tall
Needles ¹/₂ ins long

Sitka Spruce

Sitka Spruces are the biggest spruces in the world and are felled for their timber. The Sitka is one of the prickliest spruces. Its needles are hard and stiff and have sharp spines. Look too for its scaly, gray bark and small cones with papery scales.

Native to West Coast of North America
Grows up to 300 ft tall
Needles 1¹/₂ ins long

Trees & People

We need trees. They are as important to us as to the animals that live in them. Their roots cling to the soil around them and stop it being blown away. They drink in huge quantities of water and slowly release it back into the air. They help to clean the air in towns and cities and, in addition to all that, they add beauty to our lives.

But trees are in danger everywhere, not just in the tropical rain forest. In the northwestern US, whole forests of native trees have been cut down in the last twenty years for lumber. Planting trees that will be allowed to grow for hundreds of years is one of the most important things we can do for the future.

Befriend a tree

You can make a record of all the different kinds of trees you recognize or you can concentrate on just one tree, using many of the activities in this book to get to know it really well (see opposite).

You can also help to save trees by recycling paper and buying products that encourage the continued growth of rain forest trees.

Acid Rain

Carbon dioxide is only one of several waste gases that automobiles, factories and power stations release into the air. Many of these gases are acid and combine with the water in the air to produce acid rain.

Wind and air currents can carry acid rain clouds for hundreds of miles before they fall as rain. Acid rain has killed over 15 per cent of the forests in Europe. They are often far away from the cities and factories that produced the poisonous gases.

Acid rain slowly kills the leaves. With fewer leaves the tree makes less food (see page 30) and so, slowly, it begins to die. It also harms birds, fish, and insects.

Testing for acid rain

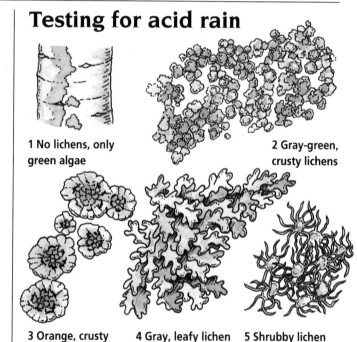

1 No lichens, only green algae

2 Gray-green, crusty lichens

3 Orange, crusty lichens

4 Gray, leafy lichen

5 Shrubby lichen

Lichens are very simple plants which grow on the bark of trees and stones. They are very sensitive to air pollution. Look at the lichens growing in your area and compare them with the pictures above. #1 is from a high pollution area, but #5 is from an area that has hardly any pollution at all.

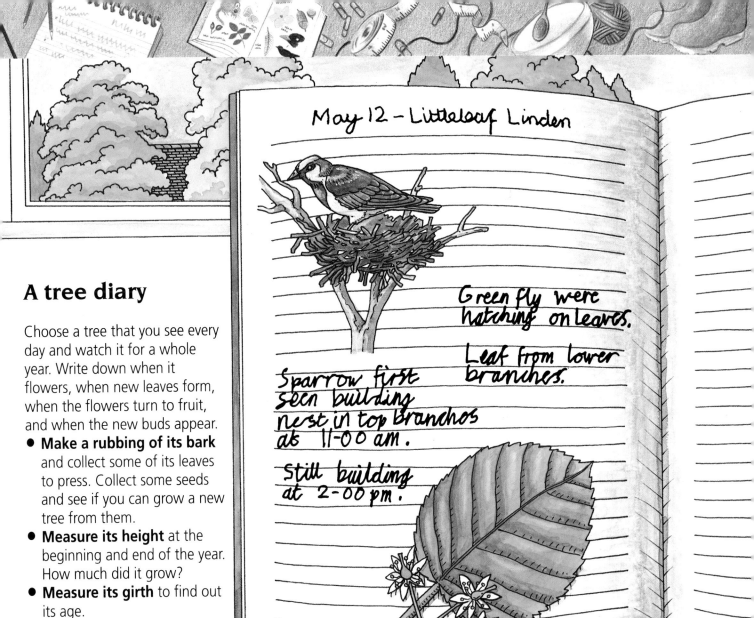

May 12 – Littleleaf Linden

Green fly were hatching on leaves.

Leaf from lower branches.

Sparrow first seen building nest in top branches at 11·00 am.

Still building at 2·00 pm.

A tree diary

Choose a tree that you see every day and watch it for a whole year. Write down when it flowers, when new leaves form, when the flowers turn to fruit, and when the new buds appear.

- **Make a rubbing of its bark** and collect some of its leaves to press. Collect some seeds and see if you can grow a new tree from them.
- **Measure its height** at the beginning and end of the year. How much did it grow?
- **Measure its girth** to find out its age.
- **Look for birds, insects, and other animals** which use the tree for food or shelter.

Recycling paper

By recycling paper, you save living trees from being cut down to make new paper. Collect cardboard, newspapers, and other good quality waste paper, and take it regularly to be recycled.

Ask your parents and school to buy products made from recycled paper as much as possible.

Two-needled Pines

Pine trees are easy to recognize from their long, thin needles, which grow in bundles of two, three, or five. The trees on these two pages all have two needles in each bundle. Look at the shape of the tree and the cones to tell them apart.

Austrian Pine

In Europe this tree is called Black Pine. You can recognize it from its scaly, black bark, its thick, spreading branches and rounded crown. Its dark green needles are stiff and shiny, and are clustered thickly and evenly around the stem. Austrian Pine makes a good town tree. It is tough and fast-growing, and does not mind city smoke and dust.

Introduced from central and southern Europe
Planted in eastern and western Canada and across US
Grows up to 60 ft tall
Needles 3½–6 ins long

Lodgepole Pine

Lodgepole Pines and Shore Pines both have prickly cones. Shore Pines are usually small, bushy trees that grow along the coast. Lodgepoles are taller and grow inland in the mountains. The prickly cones stay closed on the tree for up to twenty years until a fire sweeps through the area. Then the cones open and a new generation of trees grows.

Native to West Coast and Rocky Mountains
Grows up to 100 ft tall
Needles 2½ inches long

Red Pine

Red Pine has reddish bark like that of Scots Pine. Look at its needles to tell them apart. Red Pine's needles are longer and smell of lemons when you crush them. It is sometimes called Norway Pine, but this is a confusing name for a native tree. It probably arose because early explorers confused it with the Norway Spruce.

Native to southeastern Canada and northeastern US
Grows up to 80 ft tall
Needles 4½–6½ ins long

Scotch Pine

You can tell Scotch Pine from other pines (except Red Pine) by its dark red or pink bark, and its short, twisted pairs of blue-gray needles. Look too for its small, knobbly cones. It is grown for shelter, as an ornamental tree, and for Christmas trees.

Introduced from Europe and Asia
Now grows wild in southeastern
Canada and northeastern US
Grows up to 70 ft tall
Needles 1$\frac{1}{2}$–2$\frac{3}{4}$ ins long

Jack Pine

Jack Pines have very short, shiny-green needles. The long cones end in a curved point. They have no prickles but stay closed on the tree for many years. Like Lodgepole Pines, they are released and grow after a forest fire has burnt the parent trees. You can tell them from Lodgepole Pines because the cones point outward, whereas those of Lodgepole point inward.

Native to Canada and northern US
Grows up to 70 ft tall
Needles $\frac{3}{4}$–1$\frac{1}{2}$ ins long

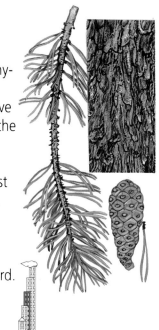

Spruce Pine

Spruce Pine has roundish cones and thin, bendy needles. Notice its pale gray bark. It is smooth on young trees, but becomes darker and furrowed on older trees.

Native to southeastern US
Grows up to 50 ft tall
Needles up to 1$\frac{1}{2}$ ins long

Bishop Pine

You can recognize Bishop Pine from its wide, domed crown and heavy branches. The tree is usually thick with cones. They are even spikier than those of Lodgepole and stay closed for more than sixty years.

Native small groups by
the coast in California
Grows up to 100 ft tall
Needles 6 ins long

Three-needled Pines

The pine trees on these two pages have needles mainly in bundles of three.

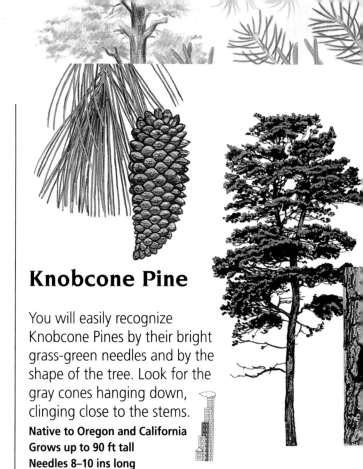

Ponderosa Pine

Ponderosa Pine is the most common pine in the Rocky Mountains. Until many were cleared for logging, grazing, or by fire, leaving instead vast areas of semi-desert and scrub, it used to be more common. This is a handsome tree with long needles. Most of them grow in bundles of three, but some grow in pairs. The bark is pinky-brown and flakes off in lobed pieces that look like the pieces of a jigsaw puzzle. Look for them under the tree. The prickly cones are about 4–5 inches long.

Native to Rocky Rocky Mountains into southern Canada
Grows up to 220 ft tall
Needles up to 9 ins long

Knobcone Pine

You will easily recognize Knobcone Pines by their bright grass-green needles and by the shape of the tree. Look for the gray cones hanging down, clinging close to the stems.

Native to Oregon and California
Grows up to 90 ft tall
Needles 8–10 ins long

Monterey Pine

Monterey Pine has bright green needles, but from a distance the whole tree looks nearly black. The large cones may stay on the tree for twenty years.

Native to California in small groves near the coast
Grows up to 130 ft tall
Needles 6 ins long

Shortleaf Pine

Like Ponderosa Pine, the needles of Shortleaf Pine grow in pairs as well as in bundles of three. They are much shorter than those of Ponderosa Pine, however. Shortleaf Pine is cut for its timber. The wood is used in construction, for plywood, and for making paper.

Native to southeastern US
Grows up to 100 ft tall
Needles 2–4 ins long

Pinyon Pine

Pinyons are small, bushy trees with big cones. Some pinyons have needles in bundles of three, while others have pairs of needles. The cones have few scales, but large seeds. The pine nuts that we eat are the seeds of the pinyon pine.

Native to southwestern US
Grows up to 30 ft tall – Needles 2 ins long

Pitch Pine

You can tell Pitch Pine from other pines by the tufts of needles which sprout from its trunk. Its yellow-green needles are stiff and twisted. Pitch Pines are now cut for their timber and for their pulp, which is made into paper. They were once valued for their resin. Colonists made turpentine, tar, and axle grease from them. They also made torches by fastening pitch pine knots to the top of poles.

Native to northeastern US
Grows up to 60 ft tall
Needles 3–5 ins long

Loblolly Pine

You may see this tree growing alongside the road or in plantations where it is cut for its timber and for making into paper. "Loblolly" means mud puddle and you will see this tree growing in wetter ground than other pines. Its thick bark is blackish-gray with deep, scaly ridges. Its cones open on the tree. They have short stalks and sharp, spreading spines.

Native to southeastern US
Grows up to 100 ft tall
Needles 5–9 ins long

Five-needled Pines

The trees on these two pages have needles in bundles of five.

Sugar Pine

The Sugar Pine is the tallest pine in the world and produces the largest cones, up to 2 feet long. The bark is usually orange-pink with small, plate-like scales. Like the White Pines (opposite), many trees are killed by blister rust.

Native to Oregon and California
Grows up to 220 ft tall
Needles 4 ins long

Limber Pine

This tall, slender, many-topped pine grows high in the Rocky Mountains. The young shoots are so bendy, you can tie them in knots without breaking them. The cones are 10 inches long and turn green and purple as they ripen. Open one up to see the black or dark red-brown seeds on short wings.

Native to Rocky Mountains
Up to 50 ft tall
Needles 3½ ins long

Bristlecone Pine

This pine grows on the east side of the Rocky Mountains. It is sometimes called the "Foxtail" Pine because its needles are pressed close to the shoot and so look like a fox's tail. Look for the many white speckles of resin on the tufts of five needles. The needles stay on the tree for up to 12 years.

Native to the Rocky Mountains
Grows up to 80 ft tall
Needles up to 1½ ins long

Whitebark Pine

Like the Limber Pine, Whitebark Pines grow high in the mountains. You can tell them apart by their cones. Those of the Whitebark Pine are short and squat. They do not open, but break up and fall off the tree.

Native to the Rocky Mountains
Grows up to 50 ft tall
Needles up to 3½ ins long

Western White Pine

Western White Pine has much longer cones than Eastern White Pine. They are 14 inches long and slightly curved. If you can, look closely at the shoots. They are thinly covered with fine, brown hairs. The bark is gray-green and on young trees it is smooth. On older trees it is smooth at the top, but covered with shiny brown, black, or red-brown scales lower down. Many older trees are killed by a fungal disease called blister rust.

Native to West Coast and western mountains
Grows up to 220 ft tall
Needles 4 ins long

Eastern White Pine

This is the only five-needled pine found east of the Rocky Mountains and is the state tree of Maine. It used to be the largest conifer in the northeast, with some trees growing up to over 200 feet. Now that the old trees have been cut down, you are most likely to see younger trees growing in plantations. The needles are blue-green and the long, narrow cones are yellow-brown.

Native to eastern Canada and northeastern US
Grows up to 100 ft tall
Needles 2½–5 ins long

Find Out Some More

Useful Organizations

Across the United States, some of the finest forests are contained in the National Forest system. State and provincial parks and forests also harbor many of the best stands of trees. Check with your school or local public library for the address of the correct agency. Many also maintain a listing of state "champion trees,"—the largest of their species—with directions for those accessible to the public.

For a listing of all **national forests** and their addresses, write to: Office of Information, U.S. Forest Service., Department of Agriculture, P.O. Box 2417, Washington DC 20013, (202) 447–3957. For **national parks**, write to: Office of Information, National Park Service, Dept of the Interior, Room 3043, Washington DC 20240.

The goal of the **Nature Conservancy** is to preserve unique and threatened habitats, many of them forested. Write to: Nature Conservancy, Suite 800, 1800 N. Kent Street, Arlington, VA 22209.

The **National Arbor Day Foundation** is dedicated to the planting and preservation of trees, from street trees to tropical forests. Write to: National Arbor Day Foundation, 100 Arbor Avenue, Nebraska City, NE 68410.

The **American Forestry Association**'s objective is proper management of forest lands; the group publishes *American Forests* magazine. Write to: American Forestry Association, 1516 P st., NW, Washington DC 20005, (202) 667–3300.

In Canada, the **Canadian Botanical Association** is the best starting point. Write to: Canadian Botanical Association, Dept. of Botany, University of British Columbia, Vancouver, British Columbia V6T 2B1.

Places To Visit

The proper name for a garden specializing in trees and shrubs is an "arboretum." They are the best place to see unusual and exotic trees. You can find out if there is one near you by asking your local library. However, you should look in your local parks and streets as well. Unusual trees are often planted there, and in the grounds of public buildings, like universities and hospitals.

In the mountains of the **East** large tracts of woodland are the rule, not the exception; especially good areas of hardwood can be found in the White Mountain and Green Mountain National Forests of New England, and the Adirondack Forest Preserve in New York. The Pine Barrens of New Jersey are one of the most unusual forest communities in North America.
The southern Appalachians also hold fine stands of hardwoods, especially Great Smokies National Park in Tennessee and North Carolina. Also in western North Carolina, the Joyce Kilmer Memorial Forest, part of Nantahala National Forest, preserves one of the largest tracts of virgin hardwoods left in the East.

Subtropical forest is restricted in the United States to **Florida**; the best place to see it is Everglades National Park. Ancient baldcypress forests can be found at Corkscrew Swamp Sanctuary, also in Florida.

North America's biggest trees are in the **West**, in California, especially the giant sequoias in Sequoia National Park. Towering coast redwoods are also found in Redwood National Park and Muir State Park. Temperate rain forest with huge Sitka spruce and western red cedar can be found in Olympic National Park and Olympic National Forest in Washington state.

Index & Glossary

To find the name of a tree in this index, search under its main name. So, to look up Sugar Maple, look under Maple, not under Sugar.

A
Alder, Speckled, 10
Apple, Pillar, 36
Arborvitae, Oriental, 61
Ash, Black, 25
Ash, Green, 25
Ash, Oregon, 25
Ash, White, 25
Aspen, Quaking, 13

B
Basswood, 11
Beech, American, 11
Beech, Purple, 11
Birch, Gray, 10
Birch, Paper, 10
Box, 51
bract: a modified and often scale-like leaf found at the base of a flower or fruit 15, 64
broad-leaved: trees that have broad, flat leaves 8–62
Buckeye, Ohio, 24
Buckeye, Yellow, 24
burr: a roundish growth, like a wart, on a tree's trunk 18

C
canopy: the extent of the branches of a tree 75

Catalpa, 36
Catalpa, Southern, 43
catkin: a drooping cluster of flowers 10
Cedar, Alaska, 63
Cedar, Atlantic White, 63
Cedar, Atlas, 67
Cedar, Deodar, 67
Cedar, Incense, 62
Cedar, Northern White, 61
Cedar, Port Orford, 63
Cherry, Black, 38
Cherry, Japanese "Kanzan", 39
Cherry, Japanese "Shirotae", 39
Cherry, Pin, 38
Cherry, Weeping Rosebud, 39

Chestnut, American, 21
Chinkapin, Golden, 51
Chokecherry, 38
Coffeetree, Kentucky, 29
conifer: trees that have long, hard leaves (needles) and produce cones for fruit, usually *evergreen* 64–77
Cottonwood, Eastern, 13
Crab Apple, Japanese, 37
Crab Apple, Prairie, 36
Crab Apple, Purple, 37
Crab Apple, Sweet, 36
Crapemyrtle, 44
Cucumbertree, 42
Cypress, Bald, 65
Cypress, Italian, 62
Cypress, Leyland, 63
Cypress, Monterey, 62

Cypress, Smooth, 62
Crab, Hupeh 40
Crab, Japanese 40
Crab, Purple 40
crown: the mass of branches and twigs at the top of the tree 7, 19, 77
crinkly: twisted leaves, as in the Holly 52
Cypress, Lawson 61
Cypress, Leyland 61
Cypress, Sawara 60
Cypress, Nootka 61
Cypress, Swamp 71, 73

D
deciduous: a tree that sheds its leaves in the autumn and is leafless for part of the year 8, 70
Dogwood, Flowering, 44

E
Elder, Box, 22
Elm, American, 12
Elm, Cedar, 12
Elm, Chinese, 45
Elm, Siberian, 45
Elm, Slippery, 12
Eucalyptus, Bluegum, 52
Eucalyptus, Red Gum, 52
evergreen: a tree which sheds and replaces its leaves gradually all the year round and is never leafless 25, 50, 52–63

F
Fig, 34
Fir, Balsam, 66
Fir, Chinese, 64
Fir, Douglas, 67

Useful Books

Eastern Trees and *Western Trees*, George A. Petrides (Houghton Milflin Co., 1988 and 1992) Comprehensive field guides to all the tree species of North America.
Peterson First Guide: Trees, George A Petrides (Houghton Mifflin Co., 1993) Simplified condensation of the previous two books, covering 243 of the most common species.
Natural History of Trees of Eastern and Central North America and *Natural History of Western Trees*, Donald Culross Peattie (Houghton Milflin Co., 1991 rev. ed) Classics of natural history writing.
Ecology of Eastern Forests and *Ecology of Western Forests*. John C. Kricher (Houghton Mifflin Co. 1988 and 1993). How forests and their components work; for older children and adults.

Index & Glossary

V

varigated: leaves with more than one colour, such as 'Golden King' Holly 52

veins: the ribs of the leaf 39

W

Y